C000319471

COOKING AROUND THE WORLD WITH Weight Watchers

For information about the Weight Watchers classes,
contact:
Weight Watchers UK Limited
11 Fairacres
Dedworth Road
Windsor
Berkshire SL4 4UY
Telephone: Windsor 856751

Art Director: Roger Judd
Photography: Barry Bullough
Home Economist: Ann Page-Wood

Line Drawings: Hayward Art Group

British Library Cataloguing in Publication Data
Cooking around the world with Weight
Watchers.
1. Reducing diets—Recipes
I. Weight Watchers
641.5′635 RM222.2
ISBN 0-450-39992-3

First published in Great Britain in 1986 by New English Library, Mill Road, Dunton Green, Sevenoaks, Kent, a division of Hodder & Stoughton Ltd.

Photoset by Rowland Phototypesetting Limited, Bury St Edmunds, Suffolk
Printed and bound by Hazell, Watson & Viney Ltd, Member of the BPCC Group, Aylesbury, Bucks.

COOKING AROUND THE WORLD

WITH

Weight Watchers*

NEW ENGLISH LIBRARY

A NOTE FROM WEIGHT WATCHERS

Weight Watchers was founded in May 1963 in New York by Jean Nidetch. Four years later, Weight Watchers was started in Britain by Bernice Weston. The first Weight Watchers class in Britain was opened in Datchet, near Windsor, in March 1967. There are now over 2,000 weekly classes held in Britain.

Weight Watchers International now offers help in some 16,500 weekly classes throughout the world, at which over 9 million men, women and children have so far enrolled.

The main purpose of Weight Watchers classes is to help members lose excess weight and learn how to keep it off for life. This is achieved through a nutritionally sound and scientifically developed dietary plan, reinforced by a system of behaviour modification, the Self Management Plan, and other time-tested factors.

In January 1985, Weight Watchers introduced its newest weight control programme which is very attractive and flexible. QUICK START is a revolutionary step for the organisation. The members are offered an accelerated three-week diet plan which enables them to lose weight approximately 20% faster than was possible on the previous plan.

The new four-way approach comprises the Food Plan, the Self Management Plan, Group Support and Exercise which combine to help the individual lose weight successfully. The new Programme has been structured with ten steps that offer built-in rewards to carry the dieter through any problem spots.

Weight Watchers continues to recognise and stress the importance of the Maintenance Plan. Learning to maintain weight loss is the fundamental core of the Weight Watchers Programme. The guidance given in 'The Maintenance Plan of a Lifetime' handbook along with Lifetime Membership of Weight Watchers will ensure that all members have the help, advice and support needed to stay at their goal.

For information about Weight Watchers classes, please ring Windsor 856751, or look in the Yellow Pages under 'Health Clubs' for the number of the local representative.

Weight Watchers Magazine* is published bi-monthly and is on sale at newsagents.

CONTENTS

INTRODUCTION

Have you ever wished you could eat things like Paella, Spaghetti Bolognese or Summer Fruit Pudding without any guilt at all? Have you ever thought that sauces, exotic recipes and scrumptious desserts were not for you on a diet? We all have! But luckily, the truth is that good food does not have to be too rich, and many foreign and British dishes can be adapted to make them acceptable in any weight reduction programme.

At Weight Watchers we know what it means to be able to enjoy a change from 'ordinary food'; we know that no matter how much care people take in choosing the 'right' food, wholesome and nutritious, they still fancy a change from time to time. Dishes from around the world can provide much-needed breaks from our usual fare, which is why many of us pop down to the local take-away or foreign restaurant so often! However, the temptation is great to indulge in rich concoctions prepared with only authenticity in mind, and one trip to a restaurant can sometimes mean disappointment at the weekly weigh-in; a high price to pay for what is after all a legitimate desire for variety and originality in our menus.

So why not instead explore the pages of this book and see what delicious foods you could eat from our extensive choice of fourteen different areas of the world? They have all been created to be low in calories but full of taste!

Because most of us would be put off at the thought of preparing intricate and time-consuming dishes, we have been careful to adapt all the recipes so that even an inexperienced or very busy cook can 'have a go' with good results. All the ingredients we use are widely available in the UK and unfamiliar cooking techniques are explained in sufficient detail to be within anyone's reach.

To make this book even more special, we have given a typical menu for a complete meal at the start of every chapter. In this way, you will if you wish be able to serve an all-Chinese or all-German meal, for example, rather than just one dish. We also give you a small introduction before each recipe, to 'place' the dish within the cuisine of the country in question, and to explain what it is if the title is not a familiar one.

If you have been trying to control your weight, you will know what a blessing it is to be able to rely on a recipe to produce good food which will not 'break your diet'. This collection of dishes from all over the world will give you just that – excellent ideas and recipes which will help to make your weight loss or weight control efforts more successful because they banish boredom from your table for good!

GENERAL INFORMATION

These recipes are for everyone who enjoys food and loves to experiment in the kitchen and to taste foreign dishes. Additionally, the recipes are calorie counted and a calorie count is given for each serving.

To achieve the best results when following the recipes in this book, do keep the following points in mind when shopping, preparing or cooking.

ARTIFICIAL SWEETENERS

Many of our recipes include sweetening in the form of small amounts of sugar or honey. If you prefer to use artificial sweeteners, you may do so – the choice is yours. The correct equivalents will be listed on the packages.

SHOPPING

EGGS – They should be size 3.

FRUIT – You may choose fresh, frozen, dried or canned fruits and only use canned fruits which are packed in natural juice with no added sugar.

VEGETABLES – We have used fresh vegetables unless otherwise indicated. If you substitute frozen or canned vegetables, it may be necessary to adjust your cooking time accordingly.

MILK – Buy fresh or longlife liquid skimmed or powdered skimmed milk.

FATS AND OILS – Margarines and oils that are high in polyunsaturated fats are generally better for you. Find out which these are from the labels which will be clearly marked. When vegetable oil is called for, oils such as corn, sunflower, peanut, safflower, soybean or any combination of these can be used. Since olive oil and Chinese sesame oil have distinctive flavours, they have been specifically indicated.

WEIGHING

You must weigh or measure all the food and liquid indicated in these recipes. Accuracy in weighing leads to good weight control for yourself. Never mix metric and imperial measures in one recipe; stick to one system or the other. Use measuring jugs and spoons and a good dietary scale. Keep these on your kitchen work surface so you can check the weight of all your recipe ingredients.

Remember, one teaspoon equals 5ml and one tablespoon equals 15ml. When a recipe says a teaspoon or tablespoon it should be a level measurement. Don't forget, careless weighing and measuring adds calories, which in turn add weight.

COOKING PROCEDURES

MEAT AND POULTRY – Always buy the leanest possible cuts of meat. When a recipe calls for minced meat, buy lean casserole cuts, remove any remaining fat, and mince the meat at home.

Meat and poultry skin and all visible fat should be removed, whenever possible, before cooking.

When roasting or grilling meat, cook it on a rack so that any fat and juices drip away during cooking.

Meat shrinks when it is cooked. As a guideline, 4oz of raw meat yields approximately 3oz when cooked.

HERBS AND SPICES – The herbs used in these recipes are dried unless otherwise indicated. If you substitute fresh herbs, use approximately twice the amount that you would dried. Generally dried herbs and spices should not be kept for longer than a year. Write the date on the container at the time of purchase and check before use.

HOT CHILLI PEPPERS – These are indigenous to many of the cuisines of the world and add a typical fiery touch. They are much smaller than the 'ordinary' green, red or yellow peppers (also known as capsicum) and require special handling because their volatile oils can irritate your skin and eyes. Always wear rubber gloves when handling chilli peppers and be careful not to touch your face or eyes while working with them. Thoroughly wash everything which has come in contact with the pepper.

NOTES FOR MEMBERS OF WEIGHT WATCHERS

All the recipes in this book have been based on the Weight Watchers Full Exchange Plan and Programme Exchanges are given with each recipe. In addition, Programme Exchanges are given for the entire menu for each chapter and these will be found on pages 214–15. However, the Programme Exchange totals *do not* include drinks. If you choose to drink wine or beer, please add the Exchange value to your total.

METRIC CONVERSION TABLE

All these are approximate conversions:

LIQUIDS		SOLIDS	
½fl oz	15ml	¼oz	7g
1fl oz	30ml	½oz	15g
2fl oz	60ml	1oz	30g
3fl oz	90ml	2oz	60g
4fl oz	120ml	3oz	90g
5fl oz	150ml	4oz	120g
6fl oz	180ml	5oz	150g
7fl oz	210ml	6oz	180g
8fl oz	240ml	7oz	210g
9fl oz	270ml	8oz	240g
10fl oz	300ml	9oz	270g
11fl oz	330ml	10oz	300g
12fl oz	360ml	11oz	330g
13fl oz	390ml	12oz	360g
14fl oz	420ml	13oz	390g
15fl oz	450ml	14oz	420g
16fl oz	480ml	15oz	450g
20fl oz (1 pint)	600ml	16oz (1lb)	480g
35fl oz	1 litre	36oz (2¼lb)	1kg 80g
40fl oz (2 pints)	1 litre 200ml	48oz (3lb)	1kg 440g

AUSTRALIA AND NEW ZEALAND

Australia, not just a country but a continent in itself, reaps the bounty of both land and sea. Its extremes of temperature yield a wealth of varied produce ranging from apples, grown in the colder southern regions, to the lush tropical fruit of Queensland.

Thousands of grazing acres result in an abundance of mutton and beef, and the encircling seas offer a diversity of seafood. All these are put to tasty use in dishes inherited sometimes from Britain and sometimes from the native specialities. Sample the land–sea combinations of Carpetbagger Steak, made with beef and oysters, and Queensland Crab and Asparagus Soup.

Australians are partial to salads and make an unusual potato salad using Granny Smith apples. For a century-old treat, serve Damper Bread, which originated with 19th century 'swagmen' (vagabonds) who cooked these unleavened, round, flat cakes over campfires during their wanderings.

New Zealand, sometimes called 'the world's garden', has the sort of climate where fruits and vegetables thrive. The produce of this beautiful land, and the top quality lamb for which it is renowned, helps to make dishes which delight visitors. Here too the British culinary origins are evident, although sometimes mixed with native Maori dishes. But one of the foods for which New Zealand is now most famed came from China. Many years ago, voyagers from the Yangtze Valley introduced a fruit which New Zealanders called the 'Chinese gooseberry'. Later, in honour of New Zealand's national bird, it was renamed 'kiwi fruit'. The fruit is used not only for desserts, but also as a meat tenderiser.

A truly original dessert, the Cantaloupe Melon Pie will be the perfect complement to a 'down under' main dish, and our recipe for New Zealand Orangeade will make a delicious drink for both children and adults.

MENU

Queensland Crab and Asparagus Soup

Scallops with Kiwi Fruit Sauce

mange-touts and cauliflower

Cantaloupe Melon Pie

New Zealand Orangeade

coffee

Granny Apple Potato Salad

SERVES 4 (190 Calories per serving)

Blue cheese and apples make this a really special salad.

2 tablespoons buttermilk

2 tablespoons lemon juice

4 teaspoons low-calorie mayonnaise

1 tablespoon chopped dill

½ teaspoon salt

¼ teaspoon white pepper

2oz (60g) blue cheese, crumbled

12oz (360g) cooked potatoes, diced

2 Granny Smith apples, cored and diced

4 sticks celery, sliced

2oz (60g) boiled ham, diced

celery leaves to garnish

In a small bowl, mix together the buttermilk, lemon juice, mayonnaise, dill, salt, pepper and blue cheese. In a salad bowl, mix together the potatoes, apple, celery and ham. Pour over the dressing and toss well. Cover with clingfilm and refrigerate for at least an hour. Toss again before serving and garnish with celery leaves.

EXCHANGES PER SERVING: ½ Fat
1 Protein
1 Bread
½ Fruit
½ Vegetable
5 Calories Optional

Lamb Chops with Pineapple-Mint Sauce

SERVES 2 (335 Calories per serving)

Mint sauce, traditionally served with lamb, is enlivened with a touch of pineapple.

2 teaspoons margarine

2 teaspoons grated onion

1 garlic clove, finely chopped

1 tablespoon plain flour

4fl oz (120ml) vegetable or chicken stock

4fl oz (120ml) pineapple juice

4 teaspoons dry white wine

1 tablespoon chopped mint

1 tablespoon lemon juice

¼ teaspoon salt

pepper

4 sprigs rosemary

4 × 3-oz (90-g) lamb chump chops

2 sprigs of mint to garnish

Heat the margarine in a saucepan over a medium heat until hot and bubbling. Add the onion and garlic and saute for about 1 minute until softened. Sprinkle in the flour and stir quickly to combine. Gradually stir in the stock, pineapple juice, wine, chopped mint, lemon juice, salt and a sprinkling of pepper. Reduce the heat to low and simmer gently for 10–15 minutes, stirring occasionally until thickened.

While the sauce is simmering, preheat the grill on its highest setting. Make a slit in the side of each chop and insert a sprig of rosemary. Transfer the lamb to the grill pan rack and grill, turning once, until cooked according to taste. Allow about 4 minutes each side for rare and 6 minutes each side for medium.

To serve, place the lamb on warm serving plates, pour over the hot sauce and garnish with the sprigs of mint.

EXCHANGES PER SERVING: 1 Fat
½ Fruit
4 Protein
25 Calories Optional

Top: Granny Apple Potato Salad (p 13)
Bottom: Lamb Chops with Pineapple-Mint Sauce
Right: New Zealand Orangeade (p 23)

New Zealand Bacon and Egg Pie

SERVES 4 (425 Calories per serving)

A New Zealand version of the ever popular quiche.

FOR THE PASTRY CASE:

3oz (90g) plain flour

¼ teaspoon salt

8 teaspoons margarine

4 tablespoons low-fat natural yogurt

1 tablespoon flour for rolling out pastry

FOR THE FILLING:

2 tomatoes, peeled and cut into quarters

4oz (120g) boiled ham, diced

3oz (90g) mature Cheddar cheese, grated

3 eggs, lightly beaten

2oz (60g) skimmed milk powder, made up to 8fl oz (240ml) with cold water

salt and pepper

To prepare the pastry case: Mix together the flour and salt. Rub in the margarine until the mixture resembles coarse breadcrumbs. Mix in the yogurt to form the pastry dough. Wrap in clingfilm and refrigerate for about an hour.

Preheat the oven to 400°F, 200°C, Gas Mark 6. Sprinkle the work surface with the extra tablespoon flour and roll out the pastry to form a circle about 9–10 inches (23–25cm) in diameter. Use the pastry to line an 8-inch (20-cm) pie plate or flan case. Prick the sides and base with a fork and bake in the pre-heated oven for 10–15 minutes until light golden brown. Remove from the oven and allow to cool a little.

Reduce the oven temperature to 350°F, 180°C, Gas Mark 4. Arrange the tomato wedges in the pastry case, top with the ham and cheese. Beat the eggs, milk and a sprinkling of salt and pepper together and pour into the flan case. Return the pie to the oven and bake for 35–40 minutes until set.

EXCHANGES PER SERVING: ½ Bread
2 Fat
½ Vegetable
2½ Protein
½ Milk
45 Calories Optional

Queensland Crab and Asparagus Soup

SERVES 4 (210 Calories per serving)

A richly elegant yet delicately flavoured soup.

- 4 teaspoons margarine
- 4oz (120g) onion, chopped
- 3oz (90g) celery, chopped
- 1 small carrot, finely chopped
- 2 garlic cloves, finely chopped
- 3 tablespoons plain flour
- 1½ pints (900ml) skimmed milk
- 2 tablespoons dry sherry
- 1 bay leaf
- 1 teaspoon salt
- 1 teaspoon Worcestershire sauce
- 1 teaspoon grated lemon zest
- ¼ teaspoon pepper
- ¼ teaspoon thyme
- 6oz (180g) well drained thawed frozen white crab meat, flaked
- 6oz (180g) asparagus spears, sliced

Heat the margarine in a saucepan over a medium heat until hot and bubbling. Add the onion, celery, carrot and garlic and saute, stirring occasionally, until the vegetables soften, 2–3 minutes. Sprinkle in the flour and stir quickly to combine. Gradually stir in the milk, bring to the boil, stirring constantly until the sauce is smooth. Add the remaining ingredients, except the crab meat and asparagus, and bring to the boil. Reduce the heat, add the crab meat and asparagus and cover the saucepan. Simmer gently, stirring occasionally, until the soup thickens and the vegetables are tender, 20–30 minutes. Remove and discard the bay leaf before serving.

EXCHANGES PER SERVING: 1 Fat
1½ Vegetable
¾ Milk
1½ Protein
30 Calories Optional

Scallops with Kiwi Fruit Sauce

SERVES 4 (185 Calories per serving)

Ginger root, lime juice and lemon peel combine with kiwi fruit to make a piquant sauce.

2 tablespoons olive oil

1lb 4oz (600g) scallops

1 teaspoon finely chopped ginger root

½ teaspoon grated shallots or onion

8fl oz (240ml) chicken stock

8fl oz (240ml) dry white wine

2 tablespoons lime juice

½ teaspoon grated lemon zest

white pepper

4 teaspoons cornflour

4 teaspoons water

2 medium kiwi fruit, peeled, cut in half lengthways and sliced

Heat the oil in a large frying pan until hot and bubbling. Add the scallops and saute until lightly browned, 3–4 minutes. Remove the scallops from the pan with a slotted spoon, keep warm while preparing the rest of the ingredients.

Add the ginger and shallots to the pan and saute for 1 minute to soften. Add the chicken stock, wine, lime juice, lemon zest and a sprinkling of pepper. Stir to combine all the ingredients and bring to the boil. Blend the cornflour and water to a smooth paste in a small bowl, pour into the boiling stock and stir quickly to combine. Reduce the heat to low and simmer, stirring occasionally, until the sauce is smooth and thickened, 5–10 minutes. Stir the scallops and kiwi fruit into the sauce and cook until heated through. Serve in individual dishes or scallop shells.

EXCHANGES PER SERVING: 1 Fat
4 Protein
½ Fruit
85 Calories Optional

Top: Queensland Crab and Asparagus Soup (p 17)
Bottom: Scallops with Kiwi Fruit Sauce

Vegetable and Beef Casserole

SERVES 4 (315 Calories per serving)

A hearty casserole, full of flavour and truly warming.

1lb 4oz (600g) boneless chuck steak
10fl oz (300ml) water
4fl oz (120ml) dry red wine
1 bay leaf, broken in half
¼ teaspoon thyme
¼ teaspoon marjoram
¼ teaspoon salt
4 teaspoons vegetable oil
8oz (240g) onions, thinly sliced
4 teaspoons plain flour
pepper
4oz (120g) carrots, sliced
4oz (120g) celery, cut in chunks

Place the steak on the rack of a grill pan. Grill, turning once, until rare. Cut into 1-inch (2.5-cm) cubes. Mix together 4fl oz (120ml) water, the wine, herbs and salt, stir in the cubed steak and cover with clingfilm. Refrigerate for at least 8 hours.

Preheat the oven to 350°F, 180°C, Gas Mark 4. Using a slotted spoon, remove the steak from the marinade, reserving the marinade. Heat the oil in a large frying pan, add the onions and meat and saute until the onions are browned, 2–3 minutes. Transfer the meat and onions to a casserole and set aside. Sprinkle the flour into the pan juices in the frying pan and cook, stirring, until the flour is lightly browned. Gradually stir in the marinade, a sprinkling of pepper and the remaining water and bring to the boil, stirring all the time. Pour into the casserole, cover and cook in the preheated oven for 1 hour. Stir in the carrots and celery, cover the casserole once again and return to the oven for an hour longer or until the meat is tender. Remove the bay leaf before serving.

EXCHANGES PER SERVING: 4 Protein
1 Fat
1½ Vegetable
35 Calories Optional

Carpet-bagger Steak

SERVES 4 (220 Calories per serving)

A traditional Australian recipe, steak stuffed with oysters.

1lb 2oz (540g) rump or fillet steak, cut in one piece about 2 inches (5cm) thick

3oz (90g) drained canned smoked oysters

1 tablespoon chopped chives

salt and pepper

2 teaspoons vegetable oil

Slit the steak horizontally from one side almost to the other. Mix the smoked oysters and chives together and season well with salt and pepper. Spread the oyster mixture inside the steak and, using thin string, sew the steak back together again.

Preheat the grill on its highest setting and place the meat on the grill pan rack. Brush the top of the steak with 1 teaspoon oil and grill for 5–6 minutes, turn the steak over, brush with the remaining oil and grill for a further 5–6 minutes on the highest setting. Reduce the heat of the grill and continue cooking, turning at least once more, until the meat is cooked according to taste, about 15 minutes or longer. Remove the string before serving.

EXCHANGES PER SERVING: 4 Protein
½ Fat
15 Calories Optional

Damper Bread

EXCHANGES PER SERVING: 1 Bread
½ Fat
15 Calories Optional

SERVES 12 (140 Calories per serving)

This bread may be frozen whole or wrapped individually in slices for single portions.

12oz (360g) plain flour

2 teaspoons baking powder

¼ teaspoon salt

6fl oz (180ml) buttermilk

2 eggs, beaten

2 tablespoons margarine, melted

Line a 1lb loaf tin with baking parchment. Preheat the oven to 350°F, 180°C, Gas Mark 4.

Sieve the flour, baking powder and salt together into a mixing bowl. Beat in the buttermilk, eggs and margarine to make a smooth batter. Pour the batter into the prepared tin and bake in the preheated oven for 45–50 minutes. Test to check the bread is cooked by inserting a metal skewer into the centre of the bread. If it comes out clean it is cooked; if not, return to the oven and test once again after a few minutes. Remove the bread from the tin and leave to cool on a wire rack. To serve, cut into twelve equal slices.

New Zealand Orangeade

SERVES 4 (105 Calories per serving)

This is especially delicious when made with freshly squeezed orange juice.

10fl oz (300ml) concentrated or freshly squeezed orange juice

2 tablespoons grated orange zest

2 tablespoons lemon juice

1 teaspoon grated lemon zest

4 teaspoons honey

½ teaspoon ground ginger

½ teaspoon ground cinnamon

4 whole cloves

1 pint (600ml) soda water or sparkling mineral water

ice cubes

Place the orange juice, orange zest, lemon juice, lemon zest, honey and spices in a saucepan. Heat through then leave to cool. Sieve the liquid into a large jug, discard the solids, cover and chill the liquid for at least 30 minutes. Chill four large glasses. Pour the soda or mineral water into the jug and stir to combine. Serve in chilled glasses with ice cubes.

EXCHANGES PER SERVING: 2 Fruit
45 Calories Optional

Cantaloupe Melon Pie

SERVES 6 (220 Calories per serving)

Try this uniquely different dessert from New Zealand.

FOR THE PASTRY:

3oz (90g) plain flour

¼ teaspoon salt

8 teaspoons margarine

4 tablespoons low-fat natural yogurt

1 tablespoon flour to roll out pastry

FOR THE FILLING:

2 tablespoons cornflour

2 tablespoons water

1 teaspoon gelatine

3 eggs, separated

3 tablespoons caster sugar

2 tablespoons lemon juice

½ teaspoon grated lemon zest

6fl oz (180ml) steaming hot water

1½ medium cantaloupe melon, diced

To prepare the pastry: Preheat the oven to 400°F, 200°C, Gas Mark 6. Mix the flour and salt together in a mixing bowl. Rub in the margarine until the mixture resembles coarse breadcrumbs. Mix in the yogurt to form the pastry dough. Refrigerate for an hour. Use extra tablespoon of flour to flour board and sprinkle on dough before rolling. Form a circle ⅛ inch (3mm) thick. Use the pastry to line an 8–9-inch (20–23-cm pie plate or flan dish. Using a fork, prick the sides and base of the pie and bake for 10–15 minutes until lightly browned. Transfer to a wire rack and leave to cool.

To prepare the filling: Blend the cornflour and water together, pour into the top of a double saucepan, sprinkle in the gelatine and leave for a few minutes to soften. Using a wire whisk, add the egg yolks, sugar, lemon juice, lemon zest and gradually whisk in the steaming hot water. Stir constantly until the mixture thickens, about 10 minutes. Remove from heat to cool.

Fold ¾ of the melon cubes into the cool egg yolk mixture. In a clean mixing bowl whisk the egg whites until peaking, gently fold into the egg yolk mixture with a metal spoon. Transfer the filling to the cool pastry crust, refrigerate for at least 3 hours until set. Before serving, arrange the remaining melon over the surface of the pie.

EXCHANGES PER SERVING: ½ Bread
1 Fat
½ Protein
½ Fruit
90 Calories Optional

BELGIUM, THE NETHERLANDS AND LUXEMBOURG

Although comparatively small in terms of square miles, the three countries of Belgium, the Netherlands and Luxembourg have produced varied and classical dishes worthy of mention in any book.

Among Belgium's edible credits are her superlative vegetables, including what has become known as Belgian chicory. We have used it here in the Cream of Chicory soup, Stuffed Chicory au Gratin, and in the colourful Chicory and Beetroot Salad.

A classic Belgian dish is Carbonnades. This French word originally meant meat grilled over charcoal, but today it refers to a rich beef stew made with beer.

One of the most popular dishes in Belgium, and the Netherlands too, is Waterzooi. The name means 'spouting water', but it is a stew made with either chicken (as in our recipe), or any freshwater fish.

In the hilly northern regions and in neighbouring Luxembourg, game like rabbit is plentiful. We offer in this chapter an unusual dish, Rabbit Flemish Style, richly flavoured with dried fruit.

In the Netherlands, food tends to be simply prepared and wholesome. Fish is a favourite, as well as cheese – Edam and Gouda – which appears in one dish after another, including our Fish Fillets 'Out of Oven'.

Saint Nicholas Spice Cookies are a genuine Dutch treat eaten at Christmas time which you will probably want to enjoy all the year round! Our Plum Tart is a delicious dessert which will end a meal on an elegant note, or be the ideal partner to a cup of strong black coffee as a typical continental afternoon snack.

MENU

Boerenkass Soup

Chicken Waterzooi

mange-touts and carrots

Plum Tart

coffee

white wine

Cream of Chicory Soup

SERVES 4 (175 Calories per serving)

This creamy hot soup is a Belgian variation of Vichyssoise.

EXCHANGES PER SERVING: 1 Fat
1½ Vegetable
¾ Milk
½ Bread

4 teaspoons margarine

4 × 3-oz (90-g) chicory, finely chopped

6oz (180g) leeks, finely chopped

1½ pints (900ml) skimmed milk

6oz (180g) potato, diced

salt and pepper

Heat 2 teaspoons margarine in a saucepan until hot and bubbling. Stir in the chicory and leeks and cook over a moderate to low heat, stirring occasionally, until the vegetables soften, about 10 minutes. Add the milk and potato and season well with salt and pepper. Simmer uncovered over a low heat, stirring frequently, until the potato is very soft, about 40 minutes. Stir in the remaining margarine, adjust the seasoning and serve in warm soup bowls.

Stuffed Chicory au Gratin

SERVES 2 (395 Calories per serving)

The interesting blend of flavours makes this a favourite supper dish.

2oz (60g) skimmed milk powder, made up to 12fl oz (360ml) with cold water
4fl oz (120ml) chicken stock
large pinch salt
large pinch pepper
4 teaspoons low-fat spread
2 tablespoons finely chopped onion
½ teaspoon finely chopped shallot
1 tablespoon plain flour
4 × 3-oz (90-g) chicory
16fl oz (480ml) water
5oz (150g) cooked chicken, chopped
4 × ½-oz (15-g) slices boiled ham
1oz (30g) Gruyere cheese, grated

Preheat the oven to 400°F, 200°C, Gas Mark 6.

Mix together the skimmed milk, stock, salt and pepper, put to one side.

Heat the low-fat spread in a saucepan over a moderate heat until hot and bubbling. Add onion and shallot and saute for 3–4 minutes. Stir in the flour and cook for 1 minute, stirring all the time. Remove from the heat and blend in the milk mixture. Bring to the boil, stirring constantly, reduce the heat and simmer very gently for 10–15 minutes, until the mixture is smooth and thickened.

Trim the ends of the chicory, taking care not to cut through the entire base or the leaves will separate. Bring the water to the boil, add the chicory, cover and cook until fork-tender, 8–10 minutes. Drain and rinse in cold water.

Mix the diced chicken with 2 tablespoons of the sauce.

Cut each chicory in half lengthways to within 1 inch (2.5cm) of the stem. Spread the leaves open and fill each chicory with a quarter of the chicken mixture. Wrap a ham slice round each chicory and lay seam side down in a flameproof dish about 8 × 8 × 2 inches (20 × 20 × 5 cm) in size. Pour over the remaining sauce and sprinkle with the cheese. Bake in the preheated oven until the sauce is bubbling, 10–15 minutes. Preheat the grill on its highest setting, remove the chicory from the oven and brown under the hot grill. Serve immediately.

EXCHANGES PER SERVING: 1 Milk
1 Fat
2½ Vegetable
4 Protein
15 Calories Optional

Chicory and Beetroot Salad

SERVES 2 (75 Calories per serving)

This is a refreshing combination of vegetables in a sharp mustardy dressing.

2 × 3-oz (90-g) chicory, trimmed

3oz (90g) cooked beetroot, cut into thin strips

FOR THE DRESSING:

2 teaspoons olive oil

1½ teaspoons white wine vinegar

1½ teaspoons water

¼ teaspoon Dijon-style mustard

salt and pepper

Cut the chicory into 1-inch (2.5-cm) slices. Mix the chicory and beetroot together in a salad bowl.

Whisk all the dressing ingredients together in a separate bowl or shake well in a screw-top jar. Pour the dressing over the chicory and beetroot, toss well and serve immediately.

EXCHANGES PER SERVING: 1½ Vegetable
1 Fat

Boerenkass Soup

SERVES 4 (230 Calories per serving)

This farmers' cheese-topped vegetable soup is a blend of interesting flavours from the Netherlands.

4 teaspoons margarine

3oz (90g) onion, chopped

7oz (210g) small cauliflower florets

6oz (180g) potatoes, cut into ½-inch (1-cm) cubes

2oz (60g) carrots, cut into ½-inch (1-cm) cubes

2oz (60g) celeriac, cut into ½-inch (1-cm) cubes

1¼ pints (750ml) chicken stock

3oz (90g) sliced ham, cut into four equal pieces

4 × ½-oz (15-g) slices white bread, toasted

3oz (90g) Gouda cheese, thinly sliced

Heat 2 teaspoons margarine in a saucepan until hot and bubbling. Add the onion and saute until translucent. Add the cauliflower, potato, carrot and celeriac and saute for 5 minutes. Stir in the chicken stock and bring to the boil. Reduce the heat, cover the saucepan and simmer gently until the vegetables are cooked but still crisp, 10–15 minutes. In a small frying pan heat the remaining margarine until hot and bubbling. Cook the ham until beginning to brown. To serve, pour the soup into four warm flameproof bowls, add a piece of ham to each portion of soup and top with a slice of toast and the sliced cheese. Grill for 2–3 minutes until the cheese is melted and bubbling.

EXCHANGES PER SERVING: 1 Fat
1 Vegetable
1 Bread
1½ Protein

Top: Chicken Waterzooi (p 32)
Bottom: Boerenkass Soup

Chicken Waterzooi

SERVES 4 (330 Calories per serving)

This chicken in creamed broth is our version of the classic Belgian stew.

4 × 6-oz (180-g) skinned chicken breasts

salt and pepper

4 teaspoons margarine

1 tablespoon plain flour

1 pint 4fl oz (720ml) chicken stock

2 sticks celery, thickly sliced

2 medium leeks, split in half and well rinsed

1 carrot, cut into chunks

4 parsley sprigs

6 peppercorns

ground nutmeg

2 tablespoons lemon juice

2 eggs, beaten

½oz (15g) skimmed milk powder made up to 2fl oz (60ml) with cold water

4 lemon slices and celery leaves to garnish

Sprinkle the chicken with salt and pepper. Heat the margarine in a large saucepan until hot and bubbling. Reduce the heat to low, add the chicken, cover and cook for about 10 minutes without browning. Stir in the stock, celery, leek, carrot, parsley, peppercorns and a sprinkling of nutmeg. Bring to the boil, cover and simmer gently for 35–40 minutes until the chicken is tender.

Transfer the chicken to a serving plate and keep warm. Sieve the cooking liquid, discard the solids and return the clear liquid to the saucepan. Stir in the lemon juice. Whisk the eggs and re-constituted milk together. Gradually stir the egg mixture into the broth. Return the chicken to the saucepan and stir over a very low heat until the liquid thickens slightly. Serve garnished with the lemon slices and celery leaves.

EXCHANGES PER SERVING: 4½ Protein
1 Fat
1 Vegetable
20 Calories Optional

Carbonnades de Boeuf

SERVES 4 (340 Calories per serving)

Beer adds the special touch to this traditional Belgian beef casserole.

1lb 4oz (600g) chuck steak, cut into 1-inch (2.5-cm) cubes

4 teaspoons vegetable oil

4oz (120g) onion, thinly sliced

1 garlic clove, finely chopped

4 teaspoons plain flour

8fl oz (240ml) beer

8fl oz (240ml) beef stock

2 parsley sprigs

1 small bay leaf

¼ teaspoon thyme

1 teaspoon red wine vinegar

ground nutmeg

salt and pepper

2 × 1-oz (30-g) slices white bread, lightly toasted

2 teaspoons Dijon-style mustard

Place the meat on the rack of the grill pan. Grill for about 10 minutes, turning once until rare. Preheat the oven to 350°F, 180°C, Gas Mark 4.

Heat the oil in a large frying pan over a moderate heat. Saute the onion and garlic for 2–3 minutes until the onion is translucent. Stir in the beef, sprinkle with the flour and stir quickly to combine. Cook, stirring constantly, for 2 minutes. Gradually blend in the beer and stock, herbs, vinegar and a sprinkling of nutmeg, salt and pepper. Bring to the boil then transfer to a casserole dish, cover and bake in the preheated oven for 1 hour 30 minutes or until the beef is tender.

Spread one side of the toast evenly with mustard. Cut each slice in half and lay on top of the beef casserole. Bake for a further 20 minutes uncovered. Remove and discard the bay leaf and parsley sprigs before serving.

EXCHANGES PER SERVING: 4 Protein
1 Fat
½ Vegetable
½ Bread
30 Calories Optional

Rabbit Flemish Style

SERVES 2 (335 Calories per serving)

Fruit marries well with game in this delicious rabbit stew.

4 large stoned prunes

1oz (30g) raisins

2 tablespoons dry sherry

9oz (270g) rabbit, cut into small cubes

2oz (60g) ham, chopped

½ teaspoon salt

large pinch pepper

1 tablespoon margarine

6oz (180g) peeled shallots

2 teaspoons plain flour

12fl oz (360ml) chicken stock

¼ teaspoon thyme

1½ teaspoons caster sugar

1 tablespoon water

1 teaspoon red wine vinegar

Stir the prunes, raisins and sherry together in a small bowl, set aside. Sprinkle the rabbit with salt and pepper and put to one side. Heat the margarine in a large saucepan until hot and bubbling, add the onions and saute until browned. Remove the onions with a slotted spoon and stir the rabbit into the hot margarine, stirring over a medium heat until well browned, about 5 minutes. Sprinkle in the flour and stir quickly to combine. Gradually stir in the chicken stock and, stirring constantly, bring to the boil, scraping all the particles that cling to the pan into the sauce. Stir in the rabbit, ham and thyme. Cover the saucepan and simmer gently until the rabbit is almost tender, about 1 hour. Stir the onions and the prune mixture into the rabbit stew, cover and continue simmering for 30–40 minutes. Remove the rabbit, onions, prunes, ham and raisins and keep warm, reserve the stock. In a small saucepan dissolve the sugar in the water, increase the heat and stir constantly until the sugar turns golden, stir in the vinegar and about 4fl oz (120ml) of the reserved stock. Bring to the boil. Stir in all the remaining stock and simmer for 2 minutes. Pour over the rabbit and other ingredients and serve.

EXCHANGES PER SERVING: 1½ Fruit
4½ Protein
1½ Fat
1 Vegetable
40 Calories Optional

Top: Plum Tart (p 37)
Bottom: Saint Nicholas Spice Cookies, (p 38)

Fish Fillets 'Out of Oven'

SERVES 2 (245 Calories per serving)

A fast, easy and interesting main course from the Netherlands.

8oz (240g) plaice fillets

1½ teaspoons lemon juice

2 teaspoons plain flour

¼ teaspoon salt

ground nutmeg

dill seeds

pepper

1 tablespoon margarine

1½oz (45g) lean ham, cut into two equal pieces

2 tablespoons dried breadcrumbs

½oz (15g) Gouda cheese, coarsely grated

Place the fish fillets in a bowl, sprinkle with the lemon juice and leave to stand for 15 minutes.

Season the flour with the salt and a sprinkling of nutmeg, dill seeds and pepper. Turn the fish fillets in the seasoned flour.

Preheat the grill on its highest setting.

Heat 2 teaspoons margarine in a medium-sized frying pan with a metal or removable handle. When the margarine is hot and bubbling, add the ham and saute until lightly browned. Using a slotted spoon, remove the ham from the frying pan and keep warm. Add the plaice fillets to the frying pan and cook over a moderate heat, turning once, until lightly browned. Place the ham on top of the fish, sprinkle with the breadcrumbs and cheese and dot with the remaining teaspoon of margarine. Place under the hot grill and cook until the cheese is melted and beginning to brown, about 3 minutes.

EXCHANGES PER SERVING: 4 Protein
1½ Fat
40 Calories Optional

Plum Tart

SERVES 4 (210 Calories per serving)

The pastry base can be made in advance and frozen before baking. Allow plenty of time for it to thaw before cooking.

FOR THE PASTRY CASE:

4oz (120g) plain flour

2 teaspoons caster sugar

8 teaspoons low-fat spread

1 egg, lightly beaten

grated zest of 1 large lemon

1 tablespoon flour for rolling out pastry

FOR THE FILLING:

8 medium dessert plums, stoned and cut into ¼-inch (½-cm) thick wedges

8 teaspoons low-calorie strawberry jam

To prepare the pastry case: Mix together the flour and sugar. Rub in the low-fat spread until the mixture resembles coarse breadcrumbs. Stir in the egg and lemon peel and mix thoroughly to form the pastry dough. Cover with clingfilm and refrigerate for about 2 hours. Use the extra tablespoon of flour to flour board and sprinkle on dough before rolling. Roll out and line a 7-inch (18-cm) loose-bottomed flan tin or 4 × 4-inch (10-cm) individual cases. Line the pastry case or cases with greaseproof paper and weigh down with some dried beans. Cover and refrigerate for at least 1 hour.

To complete the tart: Preheat the oven to 375°F, 190°C, Gas Mark 5. Bake the bean filled pastry case for 8 minutes, remove the beans and bake for a further 8–15 minutes. Arrange the plum wedges cut side up in concentric circles in the pastry case. Bake in the centre of the oven for a further 35–40 minutes until the pastry is browned and the plums soft. Allow to cool for 10 minutes then remove from the flan tin. Leave until completely cool. In a small saucepan, heat the strawberry jam until melted, brush the warm jam over the tart.

EXCHANGES PER SERVING: 1 Bread
1 Fat
1 Fruit
45 Calories Optional

Saint Nicholas Spice Cookies

SERVES 8 (175 Calories per serving – 4 biscuits each)

Aniseed, nutmeg, ginger and cloves give these cookies a really spicy flavour.

8oz (240g) plain flour

2 teaspoons ground cinnamon

¼ teaspoon crushed aniseed

¼ teaspoon baking powder

large pinch ground nutmeg

large pinch ground ginger

large pinch ground cloves

large pinch salt

5 tablespoons plus 1 teaspoon low-fat spread

2oz (60g) soft light brown sugar (4 tablespoons)

¼oz (7g) skimmed milk powder made up to 3 tablespoons with cold water

1 teaspoon cold water

1 tablespoon poppy seeds

Preheat the oven to 375°F, 190°C, Gas Mark 5. Reserve 2 tablespoons flour for rolling out the cookies. Sieve the remaining flour with the spices and salt. Set aside. Cream the low-fat spread with the sugar until light and fluffy. Stir in the dry ingredients alternately with the milk, mixing to form a dough (if the dough is rather dry, add a little extra cold water). Divide the dough in half. Sprinkle the work surface with some of the reserved flour and roll out one half of the dough to a rectangle measuring 10 × 6 inches (25 × 15 cm). Sprinkle with half the poppy seeds and gently press in with a rolling pin. Cut in half lengthwise, then cut each half into eight to make sixteen rectangular biscuits. Repeat with the other half of dough. Transfer the biscuits to a baking sheet and bake in the preheated oven for 12–15 minutes until lightly browned. Allow to cool for a few minutes then transfer to a cooling rack.

EXCHANGES PER SERVING: 1 Bread
1 Fat
40 Calories Optional

THE BRITISH ISLES

Traditional British cookery relies on good wholesome ingredients. Although perhaps not as sophisticated as Chinese cuisine or as elaborate as the French, it has qualities which most of us value, and is certainly easier on the cook!

How can you beat Steak and Kidney Pie with fresh young vegetables for a hearty and satisfying meal? Or how can you better the simplicity of Early Summer Pudding for a fragrant taste of home-grown berries?

As well as being dependably tasty and filling, properly cooked British dishes can be delightful and sometimes surprising to visitors to this country. Toad in the Hole and Cornish Pasties appeal to anyone and show how to blend flavours to warm any drizzly day!

The famed Scotch Broth and the delicious Leek and Potato Soup are both ideal to come back to after a long walk in uncertain weather, and who could resist hot Sultana Tea Scones with a cup of the nation's favourite drink?

The British Isles have many dishes to be proud of, from Irish Stew to Shepherd's Pie, and the one way to ensure success in preparing them is to shop for the best and freshest ingredients you can find. None of them will be expensive, but their quality will guarantee a better dish and many compliments for the cook.

If you thought that British dishes were not really worth taking much trouble over, think again, and you will be delighted as well as slimmer with our adaptations of these long-loved favourites.

MENU

Scotch Broth

Steak and Kidney Pie

runner beans and carrots with courgettes

fresh strawberries

coffee

red wine

Leek and Potato Soup

SERVES 4 (145 Calories per serving)

This warming soup has a smooth thick texture which is welcoming on a cold winter's night.

8 teaspoons low-fat spread

12oz (360g) trimmed leeks, chopped

3oz (90g) onions, chopped

12oz (360g) potatoes, diced

1 pint (600ml) vegetable or chicken stock

salt and pepper

grated nutmeg to garnish

Heat the low-fat spread in a saucepan until hot and bubbling, add the leeks and onion and saute for a few minutes until the vegetables begin to soften. Stir in the potatoes and stock and bring to the boil, cover the saucepan and reduce the heat to allow the soup to simmer gently for about 40 minutes. Reserve a few rings of leek for garnish. Transfer the soup to a food processor or blender and process until smooth. Return to the saucepan and reheat. Add salt and pepper to taste and pour into warm soup bowls. Sprinkle with grated nutmeg, garnish with reserved leek rings before serving.

EXCHANGES PER SERVING: 1 Fat
1½ Vegetable
1 Bread

Scotch Broth

SERVES 4 (170 Calories per serving)

A traditional hearty soup thickened with pearl barley.

8oz (240g) boned leg or shoulder of lamb

2¼ pints (11 250ml) vegetable or chicken stock

1 teaspoon salt

3oz (90g) swede, chopped

3oz (90g) leek, sliced

3oz (90g) carrot, chopped

3oz (90g) celery, sliced

3oz (90g) onion, chopped

2oz (60g) pearl barley

3 tablespoons chopped parsley

½ teaspoon pepper

Place the lamb on the grill pan rack. Grill under a medium heat, turning once until rare. Allow to cool slightly then chop into small cubes. Pour half the stock into a saucepan, add the lamb and ½ teaspoon salt. Bring to the boil, reduce the heat and partially cover the saucepan. Simmer gently for 30 minutes. Add the vegetables, pearl barley, 2 tablespoons parsley, pepper and the remaining salt and stock. Cover the saucepan and continue to simmer until the lamb and pearl barley are cooked, about 45 minutes. Ladle into warm bowls or a tureen and sprinkle with the remaining parsley.

EXCHANGES PER SERVING: 2 Protein
1½ Vegetable

Top: Irish Stew (p 45)
Bottom: Shepherd's Pie (p 46)

Steak and Kidney Pie

SERVES 4 (460 Calories per serving)

Pies are probably the longest-standing hallmark of British cookery, but we have come a long way since the days of 'raised pies' made with heavy pastry. This recipe is lighter and just as delicious.

FOR THE PASTRY:

4oz (120g) plain flour plus 1 tablespoon for rolling out

¼ teaspoon salt

10 teaspoons margarine

5 tablespoons plus one teaspoon low-fat natural yogurt

1 tablespoon skimmed milk for brushing the pastry crust

FOR THE FILLING:

2 teaspoons margarine

8oz (240g) onions, chopped

4oz (120g) mushrooms, sliced

4oz (120g) lamb's kidney, core and skin removed and cut into small pieces

1 tablespoon plain flour

10fl oz (300ml) beef stock

1 tablespoon chopped parsley

1 teaspoon thyme

1 teaspoon Worcestershire sauce

1lb (480g) cubed stewing beef, grilled until the juices stop running

salt and pepper

To prepare the pastry: Mix the flour and salt together in a bowl. Rub in the margarine until the mixture resembles coarse breadcrumbs. Stir in the yogurt and mix to form the pastry dough. Wrap in clingfilm and refrigerate for an hour or more.

To prepare the filling: Heat the margarine in a saucepan, add the onion and saute for 2–3 minutes. Stir in the mushrooms and kidney and saute for a further 2–3 minutes. Sprinkle the flour over the mixture and stir quickly to combine, stir over a moderate heat for 1 minute. Gradually blend in the stock, then stir in the herbs, Worcestershire sauce, cooked cubed meat and season with a sprinkling of salt and pepper. Bring to the boil, stirring all the time, then transfer to a deep pie dish.

To prepare the pie: Preheat the oven to 400°F, 200°C, Gas Mark 6. Use extra tablespoon flour to flour board and sprinkle on dough before rolling. Roll out pastry to form a rectangle or circle (depending on the shape of your pie dish) about 1 inch (2.5cm) larger than the dish. Cut a ½-inch (1-cm) strip off the edge of the pastry. Dampen the edge of the pie dish and press the pastry strip onto the pie dish rim. Dampen the pastry strip and lift the pie top over the meat and press the edges firmly over the pastry strip. Decorate the pastry edge and make a small hole in the top for steam to escape. If there is any pastry over, roll out some leaves or decorations for the pastry lid. Brush with the milk, then place in the preheated oven for 20 minutes, reduce the heat to 350°F, 180°C, Gas Mark 4 and cook for a further 20–30 minutes until golden.

EXCHANGES PER SERVING: 1 Bread
3 Fat
1 Vegetable
3½ Protein
30 Calories Optional

Irish Stew

SERVES 4 (395 Calories per serving)

A simple and easy-to-prepare main dish. Although traditionally an Irish stew only contains these basic vegetables, for a change add a selection of diced root vegetables.

1lb 4oz (600g) lean fillet of lamb
1 pint (600ml) chicken stock
1lb 8oz (720g) potatoes, sliced
2 medium onions, sliced
2 tablespoons chopped thyme
2 tablespoons chopped parsley
1 teaspoon salt
pepper

Trim all the visible fat from the meat and cut into bite-sized pieces, place on the grill pan rack. Grill under a medium heat, turning once, until all the juices have stopped running. Transfer the meat to a saucepan and stir in the stock, potatoes, onions, thyme, 1 tablespoon parsley, salt and a sprinkling of pepper. Cover and bring to the boil, reduce the heat and simmer gently until the meat and vegetables are tender, 30–40 minutes. Transfer to a warm serving dish and sprinkle with the reserved parsley.

EXCHANGES PER SERVING: 4 Protein
2 Bread
½ Vegetable

Shepherd's Pie

SERVES 4 (400 Calories per serving)

This recipe can be adapted to suit a vast number of different ingredients: lamb could be substituted for the beef, left over vegetables from a previous meal could be incorporated in place of the frozen mixed vegetables etc.

1 teaspoon vegetable oil
6oz (180g) onions, chopped
8oz (240g) frozen mixed vegetables
1 tablespoon plain flour
8oz (240g) canned tomatoes
4fl oz (120ml) beef stock
1lb 2oz (540g) minced beef, made into patties, grilled and crumbled
½ teaspoon oregano
salt and pepper
12oz (360g) cooked potatoes, mashed
4 tablespoons skimmed milk
2oz (60g) mature Cheddar cheese, grated

Preheat the oven to 375°F, 190°C, Gas Mark 5.

Heat the oil in a saucepan, add the onion and saute until transparent. Stir in the mixed vegetables, sprinkle the flour over and stir quickly to combine. Cook over a moderate heat for 1 minute. Stir in the tomatoes and stock, breaking up the tomatoes against the side of the saucepan. Add the minced beef and seasonings and simmer 5–10 minutes, stirring occasionally, until thickened. Beat the potatoes, milk and cheese together. Place the minced beef mixture in a deep ovenproof dish, spoon the potatoes over the top and roughen the top with the prongs of a fork. Bake in the preheated oven for 25 minutes, then place under a hot grill for 1–2 minutes to brown the potatoes.

EXCHANGES PER SERVING: 1½ Vegetable
4 Protein
1 Bread
20 Calories Optional

Top: Scotch Broth (p 42)
Bottom: Leek and Potato Soup (p 41)

John Peel.

Toad in the Hole

EXCHANGES PER SERVING: 4 Protein
1 Bread
¼ Milk
1½ Fat

SERVES 4 (535 Calories per serving)

This is always a popular family meal, enjoyed by young and old alike.

1lb 2oz (540g) beef chipolata sausages

4oz (120g) plain flour

salt

2 eggs

10fl oz (300ml) skimmed milk

2 tablespoons vegetable oil

Preheat the oven to 425°F, 210°C, Gas Mark 7. Place the sausages on the rack of the grill pan and grill under a medium heat until the fat and juices cease to run, turning once, until lightly browned. Sift the flour and a pinch of salt into a bowl, add the eggs and gradually beat in the milk to form a smooth batter.

Pour the oil into an 8 × 6-inch (20 × 15-cm) non-stick baking tin and place into the oven until very hot. Place the sausages evenly round the hot tin and pour in the batter. Bake in the preheated oven for 15 minutes, then reduce the heat to 375°F, 190°C, Gas Mark 5 for a further 10 minutes or until the batter is well risen and brown. Serve immediately.

Savoury Welsh Rarebit

SERVES 1 (310 Calories per serving)

This well known snack can easily be made into a welcome meal when accompanied by a mixed salad and followed by a choice of fresh fruit.

2oz (60g) Cheddar cheese, grated

1 tablespoon skimmed milk

1 tablespoon finely chopped onion

sage

1 teaspoon Worcestershire sauce

salt and pepper

1-oz (30-g) slice wholemeal bread, lightly toasted

TO GARNISH:

1 tomato, sliced

watercress sprigs

Mix the cheese and milk together. Stir in the onion, a sprinkling of sage, Worcestershire sauce and salt and pepper to taste. Preheat the grill on its highest setting. Spread the cheese mixture evenly onto the toast and grill until the mixture is bubbling and slightly browned. Garnish with the tomato slices and sprigs of watercress.

EXCHANGES PER SERVING: 2 Protein
1 Bread
1 Vegetable
5 Calories Optional

Cornish Pasties

SERVES 4 (330 Calories per serving)

This is a basic recipe for Cornish Pasties which can be altered to include diced swede or other root vegetables. In some parts of Cornwall the pasties are joined with the pastry fluted on the top, in other parts the pastry is fluted or flaked at one side. The choice is yours.

FOR THE PASTRY:

3oz (90g) plain flour plus 1 tablespoon flour for rolling out

¼ teaspoon salt

8 teaspoons margarine

4 tablespoons low-fat natural yogurt

1 tablespoon skimmed milk for brushing the pasties

FOR THE FILLING:

10oz (300g) lean minced beef, made into patties, grilled and crumbled

6oz (180g) cooked potato, mashed

1 onion, finely chopped

salt and pepper

To prepare the pastry: Mix the flour and salt together in a mixing bowl. Rub in the margarine until the mixture resembles coarse breadcrumbs. Mix in the yogurt to form the pastry dough, wrap in clingfilm and refrigerate for about an hour or longer.

To prepare the filling: Mix together the beef, potato and onion. Season well with salt and pepper.

To prepare the pasties: Preheat the oven to 375°F, 190°C, Gas Mark 5. Use extra tablespoon flour to flour board and sprinkle on dough before rolling. Divide the pastry into four and roll out to form four circles about 6 inches (15 cm) in diameter. Spoon a quarter of the filling into each pastry circle and moisten the pastry edge. Either fold the pastry over to join at the side or bring the pastry edges up to join on top of the filling. Flute the edges between first finger and thumb. Place the pasties on a baking sheet. Brush with the skimmed milk and bake in the preheated oven for 20 minutes, then reduce the heat to 325°F, 160°C, Gas Mark 3 for a further 15 minutes.

EXCHANGES PER SERVING: 1 Bread
2 Fat
2 Protein
½ Vegetable
30 Calories Optional

Sultana Tea Scones (p 52)

Sultana Tea Scones

SERVES 8 (220 Calories per serving)

These scones are a real treat. When you have friends coming round, make the scones just before they are due to arrive and serve them warm.

8oz (240g) plain flour plus 1 tablespoon for rolling out

4 teaspoons baking powder

4 tablespoons margarine

4oz (120g) sultanas

grated zest of ½ an orange

2 eggs

3 tablespoons skimmed milk

Preheat the oven to 425°F, 210°C, Gas Mark 7. Sieve the 8oz (240g) flour and baking powder into a bowl. Rub in the margarine until the mixture resembles coarse breadcrumbs. Stir in the sultanas and orange zest. Beat the eggs and milk together. Gradually mix in the egg and milk to form a soft dough; you will not require all the liquid. Use the remaining flour to dust the work surface and a rolling pin. Lightly knead the dough until smooth. Roll out to form a circle about 8 inches (20 cm) in diameter. Transfer the circle to a non-stick baking sheet and brush the top of the circle with the reserved egg and milk. Cut into eight wedges and bake in the preheated oven until golden, 15–18 minutes. Serve warm.

EXCHANGES PER SERVING: 1 Bread
1½ Fat
½ Fruit
20 Calories Optional

Bread and Fruit Pudding

SERVES 4 (315 Calories per serving)

EXCHANGES PER SERVING: 1 Fat
1 Bread
1 Fruit
½ Milk
1 Protein

A traditional pudding which can be made with raisins, currants or sultanas.

4 teaspoons margarine
4 × 1-oz (30-g) slices bread
4oz (120g) raisins
1 pint (600ml) skimmed milk
4 eggs, lightly beaten
artificial sweetener to taste
grated nutmeg

Spread 1 teaspoon margarine on each slice of bread. Cut the bread into small squares and layer the bread and raisins in an ovenproof dish. Warm the milk until beginning to steam, do not boil. Add to the eggs and sweeten to taste. Strain the egg and milk mixture over the bread and leave to stand 20–30 minutes. While the pudding is standing, preheat the oven to 350°F, 180°C, Gas Mark 4. Sprinkle the pudding with grated nutmeg and bake in the preheated oven for 30–40 minutes until set and lightly browned.

Early Summer Pudding

EXCHANGES PER SERVING: 1 Fruit
½ Fat
1 Bread

SERVES 4 (125 Calories per serving)

This recipe uses blackcurrants, but a mixture of brightly coloured fruits may be used, for example: raspberries, redcurrants, loganberries, blackberries.

1lb 4oz (600g) blackcurrants

3 tablespoons water

artificial sweetener to taste

2 teaspoons margarine

4 × 1-oz (30-g) slices crustless day-old bread

Place the blackcurrants and water in a saucepan and cook over a low heat until soft, sweeten to taste. Spread the margarine over the sides and base of a 1-pint (600-ml) basin. Cut the slices of bread to fit the sides and base of the basin, leaving sufficient to cover the fruit to make a 'lid'. Spoon the fruit into the bread-lined basin, cover with the remaining bread. Place a small plate or saucer that fits just inside the rim of the basin over the bread lid and keep it in position with a heavy weight. Chill overnight. To serve, turn out onto a serving plate and divide into four portions.

CENTRAL AND EASTERN EUROPE

The art of baking thrives throughout central Europe – a lure for sweet-toothed tourists. In fact, the inhabitants of the city of Budapest love pastry so much that they hold a jubilee to celebrate the anniversary of a torte!

Central and eastern European nations have a lot in common, but preserve their unique identities due to the regional variations of their agriculture and climate. Germany's staples – ham, pork and noodles – are popular everywhere, while Poland shares the Russian taste for sour cream. From the Baltic comes the abundant use of poppy and caraway seeds which adorn an array of foods, including our Liptauer Cheese, a dish popular in both Hungary and Austria.

Hungary is famed for its paprika (the Hungarian word for sweet pepper). It ranges from mild to fiery and is used in countless dishes, as in our version of Hungarian Stuffed Cabbage and Grilled Chicken Paprika.

Schinkenfleckerln, a ham and noodle casserole, is a traditional Austrian dish which is enjoyed throughout the year.

Switzerland blends the cuisine of its neighbours: France, Germany and Italy, but the food most synonymous with this country rich in dairy produce must be cheese, particularly Emmenthal. The Cheese Soup and Swiss Fondue are splendid dishes to enjoy at an informal dinner party, and you can take the 'dipping' idea straight through the meal with our dessert of Chocolate-Rum Fondue, a sure winner both with the guests and the cook!

MENU

Liptauer Cheese with celery and endives

Hungarian Stuffed Cabbage Leaves

Swiss Rosti Potatoes

Raisin Pie

coffee

red wine

Cheese Soup

SERVES 4 (185 Calories per serving)

The Swiss cheese Emmenthal gives this soup an authentic flavour.

2 teaspoons margarine
6oz (180g) onion, finely chopped
1 garlic clove, finely chopped
14fl oz (420ml) chicken stock
¼ teaspoon caraway seeds
ground nutmeg
10fl oz (300ml) skimmed milk
4 teaspoons plain flour
4oz (120g) Emmenthal cheese, grated
pepper

Heat the margarine in a saucepan until hot and bubbling. Add the onion and garlic and saute gently until the onion becomes translucent. Stir in the chicken stock, caraway seeds and a sprinkling of nutmeg. Bring to the boil, reduce the heat and simmer gently for 10 minutes. In a small bowl, blend the milk and flour together. Gradually stir the flour and milk into the stock and bring to the boil for 1–2 minutes, stirring all the time. Reduce the heat, add the cheese and stir until the cheese is partially melted. Season to taste with pepper and serve in warm soup bowls.

EXCHANGES PER SERVING: ½ Fat
½ Vegetable
¼ Milk
1 Protein
10 Calories Optional

Swiss Fondue

SERVES 4 (480 Calories per serving)

A Swiss classic, popular around the world.

6oz (180g) Brie cheese, cut into cubes

6oz (180g) Gruyere cheese, grated

2 teaspoons cornflour

1 garlic clove, cut in half

4fl oz (120ml) dry white wine

2 tablespoons dry sherry

4fl oz (120ml) skimmed milk

large pinch white pepper

8oz (240g) French bread, cut into ½-inch (1-cm) cubes and toasted

Mix together the cheeses and cornflour in a mixing bowl. Rub the inside of the top half of a double boiler with the cut sides of the garlic, discard the garlic. Add the wine and sherry and cook over hot water until the mixture begins to steam, 5–7 minutes. Gradually stir in the cheese and cornflour mixture, 3 or 4 tablespoons at a time. Cook over a medium heat, stirring constantly with a wooden spoon until the cheese is melted. Stir in the milk and pepper and cook, stirring occasionally, until the mixture is smooth. Reduce the heat to low and keep warm. To serve, let each person take 2oz (60g) bread cubes and spearing 1 cube at a time on a long-handled fondue fork, dip into the cheese mixture.

EXCHANGES PER SERVING: 3 Protein
2 Bread
50 Calories Optional

Top: Swiss Fondue
Bottom: Chocolate-Rum Fondue (p 68)

Liptauer Cheese

EXCHANGES PER SERVING: 1 Protein
15 Calories Optional

SERVES 4 (65 Calories per serving)

This spread is best prepared hours or, if possible, a day in advance. For a traditional snack, serve it with black bread and crisp raw vegetables.

8oz (240g) cottage cheese

3 tablespoons low-fat natural yogurt

2 tablespoons grated onion

1 tablespoon paprika

2 teaspoons chopped rinsed capers

1 drained canned anchovy fillet, mashed

1 teaspoon caraway seeds

1 teaspoon Dijon-style mustard

¼ teaspoon salt

large pinch white pepper

Press the cottage cheese through a sieve. Stir in the remaining ingredients and when thoroughly combined cover with clingfilm. Refrigerate for 1–2 hours, or overnight if possible, before serving.

Hungarian Sauerkraut

SERVES 2 (230 Calories per serving)

Paprika, cucumber relish and a touch of yogurt make this sauerkraut deliciously different.

2 teaspoons margarine
3oz (90g) onion, diced
2oz (60g) boiled ham, diced
2oz (60g) sliced Frankfurters
12oz (360g) drained sauerkraut
2 tablespoons cucumber relish
1 teaspoon paprika
½ teaspoon caraway seeds
2 tablespoons low-fat natural yogurt

Heat the margarine in a medium-sized saucepan until hot and bubbling. Add the onion and saute until golden. Stir in the ham and sausage, stirring over a medium heat for 1 minute. Add all the remaining ingredients, except the yogurt, and mix well. Cover the pan and simmer gently until heated through, about 10 minutes. Divide the mixture into two portions and top each serving with a tablespoon of yogurt.

EXCHANGES PER SERVING: 1 Fat
3 Vegetable
2 Protein
45 Calories Optional

Hungarian Stuffed Cabbage Leaves

SERVES 4 (230 Calories per serving)

Use only good quality meat for these cabbage rolls and serve them on a bed of sauerkraut to make a hearty main meal dish.

5oz (150g) minced pork, made into patties, grilled and crumbled

5oz (150g) minced beef, made into patties, grilled and crumbled

6oz (180g) cooked long grain rice

3oz (90g) onion, finely chopped

1 egg, lightly beaten

2 tablespoons finely chopped parsley

3 teaspoons paprika

2 garlic cloves, finely chopped

1 teaspoon salt

½ teaspoon pepper

½ teaspoon marjoram

8 large green cabbage leaves, blanched

9oz (270g) drained sauerkraut, rinsed

8oz (240g) canned tomatoes, with their liquid

10fl oz (300ml) chicken stock

Preheat the oven to 350°F, 180°C, Gas Mark 4. Mix together the pork, beef, rice, onion, egg, parsley, 2 teaspoons paprika, garlic, salt, ¼ teaspoon pepper and the marjoram. Spoon an eighth of the mixture onto the centre of each cabbage leaf, fold over the stem end, then the sides to enclose the filling. Roll each leaf tightly from the stem end to the top, tucking in the sides as you roll. Repeat the procedure with the other seven leaves.

In an ovenproof dish, about 10 × 9 × 2 inches (25 × 23 × 5 cm), mix the sauerkraut and the canned tomato liquid. Chop the canned tomatoes and stir into the sauerkraut with the chicken stock and remaining paprika and pepper. Lay the cabbage rolls, seam side down, on top of the sauerkraut, cover and bake for 50–60 minutes until the cabbage is tender and the filling cooked through.

EXCHANGES PER SERVING: 2 Protein
½ Bread
2 Vegetable
15 Calories Optional

Hungarian Stuffed Cabbage Leaves

Swiss Rosti Potatoes

SERVES 4 (155 Calories per serving)

This is a useful recipe which can be used as a side dish with a main meal or as a hearty snack topped with poached eggs.

12oz (360g) potatoes

2oz (60g) Emmenthal or Gruyere cheese, grated

2oz (60g) onions, thinly sliced

¼ teaspoon salt

¼ teaspoon paprika

pepper

2 teaspoons vegetable oil

Boil the potatoes in boiling water until just beginning to soften but still firm, about 10 minutes. Plunge in cold water and set aside to cool. Finely grate the potatoes into a bowl. Mix in the cheese, onion, salt, paprika and a sprinkling of pepper.

Heat ½ teaspoon oil in a non-stick medium-sized frying pan. Spoon a quarter of the potato mixture into the pan and, using the back of a spoon, flatten the mixture, pressing it firmly and shaping it into a circle. Cook for about 5 minutes until the bottom is golden brown, turn over and cook the other side for a further 5 minutes. Transfer to a warm plate and keep warm while repeating the procedure to make the remaining three rostis.

EXCHANGES PER SERVING: 1 Bread
½ Protein
½ Vegetable
½ Fat

Schinken-fleckerln

EXCHANGES PER SERVING: 1½ Fat
3 Protein
1 Bread
20 Calories Optional

SERVES 2 (335 Calories per serving)

In Austria, this ham and noodle casserole sometimes includes caraway seeds, and noodles in the shape of little squares are used.

1 tablespoon margarine

4 tablespoons skimmed milk

1 egg, separated

large pinch pepper

5oz (150g) boiled ham, cut into ½-inch (1-cm) cubes

6oz (180g) cooked noodles

salt

Preheat the oven to 375°F, 190°C, Gas Mark 5. Melt the margarine in a small saucepan over a low heat. Use ½ teaspoon melted margarine to grease a small casserole dish. In a small bowl combine the remaining melted margarine with the milk, egg yolk and pepper. Stir in the ham and noodles and toss well. In a separate bowl, whisk the egg white with a sprinkling of salt until peaking, gently fold into the noodle mixture with a metal spoon. Transfer the mixture to the greased casserole dish and bake in the preheated oven for 45–50 minutes until browned.

Grilled Chicken Paprika

SERVES 8 (235 Calories per serving)

Serve this Hungarian grilled chicken with noodles and a tossed green salad.

4 tablespoons margarine

4 tablespoons lemon juice

2 tablespoons paprika

2 garlic cloves, finely chopped

16 (3-oz/90-g) chicken drumsticks, skinned

6oz (180g) onion, chopped

½ small green pepper, seeded and chopped

2oz (60g) mushrooms, sliced

1 tablespoon plain flour

16fl oz (480ml) chicken stock

8oz (240g) canned tomatoes, liquidised with their juice

4 teaspoons dry sherry

Melt 2 tablespoons margarine, add the lemon juice, 2 teaspoons paprika and the garlic and stir to combine. Turn the chicken in the seasoned margarine to coat all the drumsticks, cover and leave in the refrigerator overnight to marinate.

Preheat the grill. Remove the chicken from the marinade and place on the grill pan rack. Grill for 10–15 minutes, basting occasionally with half the reserved marinade. Turn the drumsticks over and grill, basting occasionally with the remaining marinade for a further 10–15 minutes, transfer to a serving plate and keep warm. Reserve any juices in the grill pan.

Heat the remaining margarine until hot and bubbling. Add the onion and saute until translucent. Add the green pepper and mushrooms and cook, stirring from time to time, for about 3 minutes. Sprinkle in the flour and stir quickly to combine, stir over a moderate heat for 1 minute. Gradually blend in the chicken stock, pureed tomatoes, sherry and remaining paprika. Bring to the boil, reduce the heat and simmer, stirring occasionally until the sauce thickens. Stir in the reserved pan juices. Serve the sauce with the hot drumsticks.

EXCHANGES PER SERVING: 1½ Fat
4 Protein
1 Vegetable
10 Calories Optional

Raisin Pie

SERVES 6 (295 Calories per serving)

A pastry crust encases this creamy filling, flavoured with spices and raisins.

FOR THE PASTRY:

4oz (120g) plain flour

¼ teaspoon salt

3 tablespoons margarine

2 tablespoons low-fat natural yogurt

1 tablespoon flour for rolling out pastry

FOR THE FILLING:

3 eggs, separated

3 tablespoons caster sugar

1 teaspoon grated lemon zest

½ teaspoon ground cinnamon

large pinch ground cloves

4fl oz (120ml) skimmed milk

6oz (180g) large seedless raisins, roughly chopped

1 tablespoon plain flour

To prepare the pastry: Sieve the flour and salt into a bowl. Rub in the margarine until the mixture resembles coarse breadcrumbs. Mix to form a dough with the yogurt. Preheat the oven to 400°F, 200°C, Gas Mark 6. Sprinkle the tablespoon of flour onto a board and rolling pin. Roll the pastry into a 9-inch (23-cm) circle.

Use the pastry to line an 8-inch (20-cm) pie plate and flute or crimp the edges. Prick the base and sides of the pie with a fork and bake in the preheated oven for about 10 minutes or until lightly browned. Remove the pastry case from the oven and allow to cool while preparing the filling. Reduce the oven temperature to 350°F, 180°C, Gas Mark 4.

To prepare the filling: Using an electric mixer, whisk the egg yolks until light in colour. Add the sugar, lemon zest, cinnamon and cloves and continue whisking for a further 3 minutes. Stir in the skimmed milk. Sprinkle the raisins with the flour, then carefully fold into the mixture. In a separate bowl, whisk the egg whites until peaking, gently fold into the filling ingredients. Spoon the mixture into the pastry case and bake in the preheated oven for 25–30 minutes until a thin-bladed knife inserted into the middle comes out clean. Serve warm.

EXCHANGES PER SERVING: ½ Bread
1½ Fat
½ Protein
1 Fruit
70 Calories Optional

Chocolate-Rum Fondue

SERVES 6 (95 Calories per serving)

This cold fondue is suitable for a wide variety of fruits. Either use the fruits suggested in the recipe or substitute your particular favourites.

1 tablespoon cornflour

5fl oz (150ml) skimmed milk

8 teaspoons chocolate spread

3 tablespoons rum (1½fl oz/45ml)

½ medium banana, thickly sliced

1 medium apple, quartered, cored and sliced

1 teaspoon lemon juice

1 medium orange, peeled and segmented

1 medium kiwi fruit, peeled and thickly sliced

5oz (150g) strawberries

2 medium plums, stoned and cut into wedges

Mix the cornflour to a smooth paste with a little of the skimmed milk. Heat the remaining milk in a small saucepan, add the cornflour paste and chocolate spread and bring to the boil, stirring constantly. Boil for 1 minute. Remove from the heat and stir in the rum. Leave to cool, stirring from time to time to prevent a skin forming. Cover with clingfilm and refrigerate until required. Toss the banana and apple in the lemon juice. Place the chocolate sauce in a small bowl in the centre of the serving plate. Arrange all the fruits decoratively round the sauce.

EXCHANGES PER SERVING: 1 Fruit
55 Calories Optional

CHINA

In China, many foods are symbolic, so meals often have a message. For example, if you want to wish your dinner companions good health, serve them bamboo shoots. Rice, the number one accompaniment, symbolises fertility! Noodles symbolise longevity, so it's considered bad luck to break them. Because lions are believed to ward off evil spirits, the Mandarin dish called Lion's Head (pork rolled into a ball resembling the head of the king of the beasts) is very popular. Our meatless version turns that 'head' into more convenient patties and also helps ward off sad spirits at the scales!

Meatless dishes are common in China because of the use of bean curd, also known as 'tofu', which is a high protein food with a bland taste. Tofu has the advantage of taking on the flavour of the foods cooked with it, so it is very versatile and a healthy choice, too, because it is low in Calories and in sodium, and has practically no fat.

Despite provincial variations, most Chinese dishes share certain ingredients, among them fresh ginger, spring onions, dried mushrooms, cornflour, miso (fermented bean paste), and sesame and peanut oils, while soy sauce is to China what salt is to the West.

The Chinese juggle five basic flavours: salty, sweet, sour, bitter and pungent, so that no one flavour dominates. An exception is the highly spiced Szechuan cooking of the North.

The most common cooking methods are steaming and stir-frying, which depends on slicing and dicing foods into bite-size pieces, followed by swift cooking so that vegetables retain their crunchy texture.

Dessert is usually fruit, as in our Chilled Melon Bowl, invariably followed by cha (tea). For an authentic touch, wish guests 'ho yum ho sic': good drinking, good eating!

MENU

Orange Chicken

Sesame Vegetable Stir-Fry

boiled rice

Chilled Melon Bowl

China tea

Bean Curd Appetiser

SERVES 4 (135 Calories per serving)

Versatile tofu (bean curd) absorbs the flavours of this tasty sauce.

FOR THE SAUCE:

4 tablespoons soy sauce

2 tablespoons rice or cider vinegar

1 tablespoon chopped spring onions

1 tablespoon honey

1 teaspoon chilli oil*

FOR THE TOFU:

12oz (360g) firm-style tofu, drained and cut into 1-inch (2.5-cm) cubes

2 tablespoons cornflour

1 tablespoon peanut oil

In a small bowl combine all the sauce ingredients, mix well and put to one side.

Pat the tofu dry with kitchen towels. Sieve the cornflour onto a plate, turn the squares of tofu in the cornflour to coat. Heat the peanut oil in a medium-sized frying pan or wok. Add the tofu and saute over a high heat, stirring all the time, until browned on all sides. Transfer to a warm serving plate. Whisk the sauce ingredients together once again and serve immediately as a dipping sauce for the hot tofu.

EXCHANGES PER SERVING: 1 Fat
1 Protein
30 Calories Optional

*If you cannot find chilli oil in your local supermarket or in an oriental food shop, you can prepare your own, in advance to allow the flavour to develop, by using any vegetable oil with either ½ a fresh chilli pepper, seeded and chopped, or ¼ of a teaspoon of chopped dried red chilli pepper added.

Mushroom Soup

EXCHANGES PER SERVING: 1½ Protein
1 Vegetable

SERVES 4 (75 Calories per serving)

A clear soup which is simple to prepare and ideal for a snack lunch or as part of a main meal.

8oz (240g) skinned and boned chicken, cut into thin slices

1 pint 10fl oz (900ml) chicken stock

1-inch (3-cm) piece ginger root, peeled

9oz (270g) button mushrooms, sliced

3oz (90g) spring onions, sliced

salt and pepper

Place the chicken, stock and ginger in a saucepan, bring to the boil, reduce the heat, cover and simmer for 20 minutes. Add the mushrooms, cover and continue simmering for 15 minutes. Stir in the spring onions and simmer uncovered for a further 5 minutes. Season to taste with salt and pepper and ladle into warm soup bowls.

Chicken and Chestnuts

SERVES 4 (245 Calories per serving)

Chestnuts give an unusual taste to this dish.

1lb 4oz (600g) skinned and boned chicken, cut into 1½-inch (4-cm) pieces

2 tablespoons soy sauce

1 tablespoon peanut oil

1 red pepper, seeded and diced

4 tablespoons chopped spring onions

1 garlic clove, finely chopped

½ teaspoon finely chopped root ginger

12 small chestnuts, boiled and peeled

12fl oz (360ml) chicken stock

2 tablespoons dry sherry

2 teaspoons cornflour

1 teaspoon sesame oil

pepper

Toss the chicken in the soy sauce, cover with clingfilm and leave in a cool place for 30–40 minutes.

Heat the peanut oil in a wok or saucepan, add the red pepper, spring onion, garlic and ginger and saute for about 2 minutes over a medium heat. Drain the chicken, reserving the marinade, and stir a few pieces at a time into the vegetable mixture. Add the chestnuts, increase the heat to high and cook, stirring constantly, until the chicken begins to brown, about 2 minutes. Stir in the chicken stock and sherry and bring to the boil. Reduce the heat and simmer for 1 minute. Gradually blend the soy sauce into the cornflour, stir in the sesame oil and a sprinkling of pepper, pour into the chicken mixture. Bring to the boil, stirring all the time until thickened.

EXCHANGES PER SERVING: 4 Protein
1 Fat
½ Vegetable
½ Bread
15 Calories Optional

Orange Chicken

SERVES 4 (255 Calories per serving)

The orange zest gives this dish colour and piquancy. Be sure to remove all the white pith from the orange; this is easily done with a potato peeler which removes only the zest or by using a zester.

1lb 4oz (600g) skinned and boned chicken, cut into 1½-inch (4-cm) pieces

6 tablespoons dry sherry

¼ teaspoon salt

4 teaspoons peanut oil

1 small red pepper, seeded and cut into matchstick-sized pieces

2 tablespoons chopped spring onions

zest of ½ an orange, cut into 2-inch × ⅛-inch (5-cm × 3-mm) strips and blanched

1 garlic clove, finely chopped

1 teaspoon cornflour

1 teaspoon granulated sugar

1 tablespoon soy sauce

1 tablespoon water

1 teaspoon rice or cider vinegar

4 trimmed spring onions to garnish

Mix together the chicken, 3 tablespoons sherry and salt, cover with clingfilm and leave in a cool place for 30–40 minutes.

Heat the oil in a wok or medium-sized frying pan over a medium heat. Add the pepper, spring onions, orange zest and garlic and stir-fry for about 3 minutes, stirring frequently. Remove the chicken from the marinade with a slotted spoon, reserve the marinade and add the chicken to the wok. Increase the heat and continue stir-frying until the chicken is browned, about 5 minutes. Blend the reserved marinade into the cornflour and sugar. Stir in the remaining sherry, vinegar, soy sauce and water and pour into the vegetable mixture. Cook, stirring constantly, until the mixture boils and thickens. Serve garnished with spring onions.

To make 'spring onion curls' for the garnish:

- using a sharp knife, cut the root off very near the edge.
- cut the top off the onions, just where the leaves separate.
- starting near the base, make even, lengthwise cuts, close together, through the onion.
- place in very cold water for approximately half an hour.
- drain, shake off excess water and use for garnish.

EXCHANGES PER SERVING: 4 Protein
1 Fat
½ Vegetable
30 Calories Optional

Top: Chilled Melon Bowl (p 82)
Bottom: Orange Chicken

Lion's Head Casserole

SERVES 4 (230 Calories per serving)

Flavoured tofu sandwiched between layers of shredded Chinese leaves.

- 1 tablespoon peanut oil
- 1 tablespoon sesame oil
- 4oz (120g) spring onions, chopped
- 2 garlic cloves, finely chopped
- 1 teaspoon finely grated ginger root
- 15oz (450g) drained firm-style tofu
- 3 eggs, lightly beaten
- 1 tablespoon cornflour
- 1 tablespoon soy sauce
- ½ teaspoon vegetable extract
- 15oz (450g) Chinese leaves, shredded
- 8fl oz (240ml) vegetable stock
- 2 tablespoons dry sherry

Heat the oils in a medium-sized frying pan. Add the spring onions, garlic and ginger and saute until the onions have softened, about 1 minute. Mash the tofu well in a mixing bowl, stir in half the spring onion mixture, the eggs, cornflour, soy sauce and vegetable extract. Mix well to combine all the ingredients evenly.

Spread half the shredded Chinese leaves in the bottom of a large casserole. Spread the tofu mixture over the top and cover with the remaining Chinese leaves and sauted spring onions. Mix the stock and sherry together and pour over the casserole. Cook over a low heat allowing the stock to simmer gently and the tofu mixture to become firm, about 40 minutes.

EXCHANGES PER SERVING: 1½ Fat
2 Vegetable
2 Protein
15 Calories Optional

Chinese Cold Noodles in Sesame Sauce

SERVES 2 (265 Calories per serving)

Delicious peanut flavoured noodles.

3 tablespoons chicken stock

3 tablespoons crunchy peanut butter

1 tablespoon soy sauce

¼ teaspoon finely chopped ginger root

½ clove garlic, crushed

½ teaspoon sesame oil

paprika

6oz (180g) cooked thin spaghetti (vermicelli)

8 spring onions, chopped

Mix together the chicken stock, peanut butter, soy sauce, ginger and garlic. Bring to the boil, stirring frequently. Remove from the heat, stir in the oil and a sprinkling of paprika. Transfer the mixture to a small bowl, allow to cool a little, cover with clingfilm and refrigerate for at least 30 minutes. Place the spaghetti in the serving bowl, pour over the sauce and toss well. Sprinkle with the spring onions and toss once more.

EXCHANGES PER SERVING: 1½ Protein
1½ Fat
1 Bread
½ Vegetable
15 Calories Optional

Sesame Vegetable Stir-Fry

EXCHANGES PER SERVING: ½ Fat
2 Vegetable
½ Bread
30 Calories Optional

SERVES 4 (85 Calories per serving)

This is a delightful recipe; the vegetables retain their texture and the bright array of colours attracts the eye.

2 teaspoons peanut oil

4oz (120g) carrots, sliced

4oz (120g) celery, diagonally sliced

1 green pepper, seeded and cut into thin strips

1 red pepper, seeded and cut into thin strips

3oz (90g) onion, chopped

2oz (60g) cabbage, shredded

8 spring onions, diagonally sliced

6oz (180g) water chestnuts, sliced

2 tablespoons sesame seeds, toasted

Heat the oil in a wok or frying pan. Add the carrots, celery, green and red peppers and onion and stir-fry over a medium heat for 4–5 minutes until the onions and peppers begin to soften. Stir in the remaining ingredients and continue stir-frying until all the vegetables are piping hot. Do not overcook. Serve immediately.

Sweet and Sour Pork

SERVES 2 (355 Calories per serving)

This is probably one of the most popular Chinese dishes. Take care not to overcook the vegetables so they remain crisp.

10oz (300g) pork fillet

4fl oz (120ml) chicken stock

4 tablespoons soy sauce

4 teaspoons cider vinegar

4 teaspoons tomato puree

2 teaspoons vegetable oil

1 green pepper, seeded and cut into strips

4oz (120g) cauliflower florets

2oz (60g) celery, sliced

1 small onion, quartered and separated into sections

¼ small pineapple (4oz), peeled and diced

2 teaspoons cornflour

Place the pork in a shallow dish. Mix together the stock, soy sauce, vinegar and tomato puree, pour over the pork, cover with clingfilm and refrigerate for at least 2 hours. Turn the meat frequently during the marinading time.

Drain the pork from the marinade. Reserve the marinade and transfer the pork to the grill pan rack. Grill the meat, turning once until just cooked. Allow to cool a little then cut into thin slices. Heat the oil in a medium-sized frying pan or wok. Add the green pepper, cauliflower, celery and onion and stir-fry until tender-crisp. Add the pork and pineapple and stir well to mix. Blend the reserved marinade into the cornflour and pour over the pork and vegetable mixture. Stir constantly over a moderate heat until the mixture thickens and the pork and pineapple have heated through.

EXCHANGES PER SERVING: 4 Protein
1 Fat
2 Vegetable
½ Fruit
20 Calories Optional

Mandarin Almond Jelly

SERVES 4 (100 Calories per serving)

A light and delicious dessert which can be prepared in advance and stored in the refrigerator.

16fl oz (480ml) skimmed milk

1 tablespoon gelatine

4 teaspoons caster sugar

1 teaspoon almond flavouring

8oz (240g) drained canned mandarin orange segments, reserve 4fl oz (120ml) of the juice

½ teaspoon cornflour

Pour 4fl oz (120ml) of the milk into a small bowl, sprinkle in the gelatine and 3 teaspoons of sugar, stir to combine. Stand the bowl in a saucepan of gently simmering water until the gelatine and sugar have completely dissolved. Stir into the remaining milk and almond flavouring, then pour into four serving glasses or dishes, cover and refrigerate until set, about 1½ hours.

Blend a little of the reserved mandarin juice with the cornflour. Heat the remaining juice and sugar, stir in the cornflour paste and continue stirring until the mixture has boiled for about 1 minute and has thickened. Remove from the heat and stir in the mandarin segments, ensuring they are all coated with the sauce. Cover and refrigerate for about 30 minutes.

To serve, top each portion of almond jelly with a quarter of the mandarin sauce.

EXCHANGES PER SERVING: ¼ Milk
½ Fruit
40 Calories Optional

Chilled Melon Bowl

EXCHANGES PER SERVING: 1 Fruit
15 Calories Optional

SERVES 4 (50 Calories per serving)

This fruit salad is simple to prepare and looks attractive served in the melon skin.

1 medium rock or cantaloupe melon

¼ teaspoon almond flavouring, optional

1 medium orange, peeled, segmented and all membranes removed

1 medium pear, cored and cut into wedges

5oz (150g) watermelon balls

Cut a slice off the top of the rock melon. Remove and discard the seeds. Using a melon scoop or teaspoon, scoop out balls of melon flesh and place in a bowl. Sprinkle the inside of the melon with the almond flavouring. Mix together the melon balls, orange segments, pear wedges and watermelon balls. Fill the melon with the prepared fruit and chill until ready to serve. Do not prepare too far in advance or the pear may discolour.

FRANCE

With one of the world's finest cuisines, France remains a country where people are sufficiently interested in good food to adapt traditional dishes to the latest nutritional thinking: this is how the Nouvelle Cuisine was born.

So come with us to France on a cook's tour. Although the dishes vary from one region to another, certain points are national hallmarks. One is the respect and love of fresh vegetables, which are included in every meal whether in salads or cooked dishes.

French cooks are also renowned for their skilful use of seasonings, which they believe should enhance the food's natural flavour rather than overwhelm it. It is this skill which turns fish into delicacies like Salmon en Papillote, and which transforms Soupe au Pistou into an aromatic feast.

Typical of French regional cookery is the Cassoulet, a thrifty dried beans and meat stew which originated in the area around Toulouse: a wonderfully satisfying dish which can be prepared in advance because its flavour improves overnight! Another favourite French stew is Veal Marengo, a dish created by Napoleon's chef in honour of the Emperor's victory at the battle of Marengo.

But you won't have to meet your Waterloo with desserts and pastries for you can enjoy three popular choices: the Black Cherry Clafouti, a perfect dessert, the Pear Sorbet, a lovely light concoction which will refresh your palate, and the Brioches, ideal as part of a typical continental breakfast, as a snack, or as the accompaniment to a mid-afternoon cup of tea or coffee.

No French meal is considered complete without wine, but here is an international tip: your wine portion will go twice as far when mixed with soda water to make a spritzer. A votre santé!

MENU

Soupe au Pistou

Salmon en Papillote

braised lettuce

Pear Sorbet

coffee

white wine

Soupe au Pistou

SERVES 4 (135 Calories per serving)

A hearty vegetable soup laced with fresh basil, garlic and Parmesan cheese.

FOR THE SOUP:

1oz (30g) dried red kidney beans
1oz (30g) dried haricot beans
2 pints (1 litre 200ml) water
1 small onion, chopped
2 sticks celery, sliced
3oz (90g) potato, cut into ¼-inch (5-mm) dice
2 small tomatoes, peeled and chopped
1 carrot, sliced
1 small courgette, sliced
2oz (60g) green beans, diagonally sliced
1 tablespoon tomato puree
1 bay leaf
1oz (30g) macaroni
salt and pepper

FOR THE PISTOU:

6 sprigs fresh basil
1 tablespoon hot water
2 teaspoons olive oil
1 garlic clove, finely chopped
½oz (15g) Parmesan cheese, finely grated

To prepare the soup: cover beans with water and leave overnight, drain. The next day place the beans and the 2 pints (1 litre 200ml) of water in a large saucepan, bring to a rolling boil and boil rapidly for 15 minutes. Reduce the heat, add the onion and celery and simmer for 30 minutes. Add the remaining soup ingredients to the pan, except the macaroni, salt and pepper, cover and simmer for a further 45–60 minutes. Stir in the macaroni, salt and pepper and boil gently for 5–10 minutes until the macaroni is cooked.

To prepare the pistou: While the soup is cooking, place all the ingredients, except the cheese, in a small bowl and crush them to a paste with a wooden spoon until smooth.

To serve: Remove and discard the bay leaf from the soup. Divide the pistou between four warm soup bowls. Ladle the soup into the bowls, sprinkle with Parmesan and serve immediately.

EXCHANGES PER SERVING: 1 Bread
1½ Vegetable
½ Fat
10 Calories Optional

Pan Bagna

SERVES 2 (235 Calories per serving)

This sandwich Nicoise is sold along many of the streets and beaches of Nice.

2 drained canned anchovy fillets

1 teaspoon capers

¼ teaspoon thyme

pepper

1 tablespoon olive oil

2 teaspoons water

1 teaspoon red wine vinegar

2 × 1½-oz (45-g) crusty rolls or pieces of French stick

1 garlic clove, peeled

4 large fresh basil or mint leaves

½ medium tomato, thinly sliced

½ red onion, thinly sliced

2oz (60g) drained canned tuna, flaked

Using a pestle and mortar, or in a small bowl and using the back of a spoon, mash together the anchovy fillets, capers, thyme and a sprinkling of pepper to form a smooth paste. Gradually add the oil, water and vinegar, mixing well after each addition. Set aside.

Cut the rolls or bread in half horizontally. Rub the cut sides with the garlic clove. Discard the garlic. Brush the anchovy paste evenly over all the cut sides of bread. Place the bottom halves of the sandwiches on a plate. Cover with the basil or mint leaves, then the slices of tomato and onion. Spread the flaked tuna over the vegetables and press the remaining halves of the rolls or bread over the filling. Place a heavy plate on top of the sandwiches for 3–4 minutes to allow the flavours to blend and press the filling firmly together.

EXCHANGES PER SERVING: 1½ Fat
1½ Bread
½ Vegetable
1 Protein
5 Calories Optional

Top: Soupe au Pistou (p 85)
Bottom: Pan Bagna

Leeks and Mushrooms Provencal

SERVES 2 (95 Calories per serving)

This is an excellent appetiser or it can be served as an accompaniment to a main poultry or fish dish.

2 teaspoons olive oil

1 garlic clove, finely chopped

2 medium leeks, cut in halves lengthways, then into 1½-inch (4-cm) pieces

2oz (60g) mushrooms, quartered

4oz (120g) drained canned tomatoes, chopped

2 large stoned black olives, thinly sliced

1 tablespoon dry white wine

1½ teaspoons lemon juice

½ teaspoon Dijon-style mustard

¼ teaspoon mashed drained anchovy fillet (about half a fillet)

salt and pepper

Heat the oil in a medium-sized frying pan over a medium to high heat. Add the garlic and leeks and saute gently, stirring occasionally until the leeks begin to wilt, 3–4 minutes. Add the mushrooms and continue cooking for 2–3 minutes. Stir in all the remaining ingredients and cook for a further 3–4 minutes or until heated through. Adjust the seasoning and serve.

EXCHANGES PER SERVING: 1 Fat
2 Vegetable
15 Calories Optional

Cassoulet

SERVES 4 (270 Calories per serving)

This traditional French dish makes an ideal filling lunch or supper.

3oz (90g) dried haricot beans

8fl oz (240ml) water

1 teaspoon vegetable oil

1 teaspoon margarine

12oz (360g) chicken thighs, skinned, boned and cut into 2-inch (5-cm) pieces

3 whole cloves

5oz (150g) carrots, cut into 2-inch (5-cm) chunks

4oz (120g) Spanish onion, thickly sliced

2 garlic cloves, finely chopped

4 tablespoons chopped parsley

8fl oz (240ml) chicken stock

8oz (240g) canned chopped tomatoes, drained

bay leaf

4oz (120g) 'precooked' saveloys

Wash the beans, leave to soak in the 8fl oz (240ml) water overnight. The next day bring the beans and their soaking water to a rolling boil. Boil hard for 15 minutes while preparing the cassoulet.

Preheat the oven to 350°F, 180°C, Gas Mark 4. In a medium-sized frying pan heat ½ teaspoon oil and ½ teaspoon margarine until hot and bubbling. Add the chicken and brown all over in the hot fat. Transfer the chicken to a casserole dish.

Press the cloves into three chunks of carrot. Add the remaining oil and margarine to the frying pan and heat until hot and bubbling once again. Add the carrot, onion and garlic and saute, stirring occasionally until the onion slices are translucent. Transfer the vegetables to the chicken in the casserole and stir in 2 tablespoons parsley, the chicken stock, tomatoes and their liquid, bay leaf and the beans and their cooking liquid.

Using a sharp knife make ½-inch (1-cm) slashes in the sausage and place on top of the mixture in the casserole. Cover and bake in the preheated oven for 1 hour 20 minutes or until the beans are cooked. Remove and discard the bay leaf, season with salt and pepper and sprinkle with the remaining parsley.

EXCHANGES PER SERVING: 4 Protein
½ Fat
1½ Vegetable

Salmon en Papillote

SERVES 4 (410 Calories per serving)

This foil-baked salmon is an interesting blend of colours, flavours and textures.

4 teaspoons vegetable oil

8oz (240g) carrots, cut into long matchstick pieces

10oz (300g) courgettes, cut into long matchstick pieces

2 medium leeks, cut into long matchstick pieces

2 tablespoons finely chopped shallots

4fl oz (120ml) water

3 tablespoons dry sherry

2 tablespoons finely chopped parsley

2 tablespoons lemon juice

2 teaspoons grated lemon peel

2 teaspoons Dijon-style mustard

½ teaspoon salt

¼ teaspoon white pepper

4 × 6-oz (180-g) salmon steaks

Preheat the oven to 375°F, 190°C, Gas Mark 5.

In a large frying pan heat 2 teaspoons oil over a medium heat. Saute the carrots, courgettes, leeks and shallots until slightly tender, 4–5 minutes. Stir in the remaining ingredients, except the salmon, and cook, stirring occasionally, for 2 minutes.

Brush four sheets of foil, each large enough to hold a salmon steak, with the remaining oil. Place one salmon steak in the centre of each sheet of foil. Spoon a quarter of the vegetable mixture and liquid over each steak, fold over the foil and crimp the edges to seal. Place the foil packages on a baking sheet and bake in the preheated oven for 15–20 minutes until the salmon flakes when tested with a fork and the vegetables are tender. Transfer the salmon and vegetables to serving plates.

EXCHANGES PER SERVING: 1 Fat
2 Vegetable
4 Protein
15 Calories Optional

PRODUCT
MAISON FONDÉE
J. Moreau & Fils

Veal Marengo

SERVES 2 (250 Calories per serving)

Traditionally this delicious stew is served over noodles.

10oz (300g) boneless shoulder of veal, cut into 1-inch (2.5-cm) cubes

2 teaspoons margarine

1 small onion, chopped

1 garlic clove, finely chopped

1 tablespoon plain flour

6fl oz (180ml) chicken stock

4oz (120g) drained canned tomatoes, chopped

2 tablespoons dry white wine

¼ teaspoon grated lemon zest

½ bay leaf

¼ teaspoon thyme

2oz (60g) mushrooms, quartered

1½ teaspoons finely chopped parsley

salt and pepper

Preheat the grill on its highest setting. Place the veal on the grill pan rack and grill for about 5 minutes until the meat is browned on all sides. Set aside.

Heat the margarine in a saucepan over a moderate heat. When hot and bubbling, add the onion and garlic and saute, stirring occasionally, until the onion is translucent. Add the flour and cook for 1–2 minutes, stirring all the time. Remove from the heat and gradually blend in the stock. Bring to the boil, stirring constantly. Reduce the heat and stir in the tomatoes, wine, lemon peel, bay leaf, thyme and veal. Cover the saucepan and simmer gently, stirring occasionally, until the meat is tender, about an hour. Stir in the mushrooms and parsley and cook for a further 5 minutes. Season well, remove the bay leaf and serve piping hot.

EXCHANGES PER SERVING: 4 Protein
1 Fat
1½ Vegetable
30 Calories Optional

Steak au Poivre

SERVES 2 (305 Calories per serving)

No repertoire of French cooking would be complete without a traditional peppered steak.

1½ teaspoons coarsely ground black peppercorns

2 × 5-oz (150-g) boneless sirloin, fillet or rump steaks

2 teaspoons margarine

½ teaspoon salt

3oz (90g) mushrooms, sliced

1 tablespoon finely chopped shallots

2 tablespoons dry red wine

watercress or parsley to garnish

Firmly press ¾ teaspoon pepper onto both sides of each steak, leave to stand 10–15 minutes. Preheat the grill on its highest setting. Place the meat on the grill rack and grill for about 2 minutes on each side, until rare.

In a medium-sized frying pan, heat the margarine over a high heat until hot and bubbling. Transfer the steak to the frying pan and sear quickly on both sides. Sprinkle each side of the steak with salt and transfer to a warm serving plate. Keep warm while preparing the sauce.

Add the mushrooms and shallots to the frying pan, saute until the mushrooms are golden, 1–2 minutes. Stir in the wine and cook, stirring continually, until the liquid is reduced, 2–3 minutes. Pour the sauce over the warm steak and serve garnished with sprigs of watercress or parsley.

EXCHANGES PER SERVING: 4 Protein
1 Fat
1 Vegetable
15 Calories Optional

Braised Lettuce with Vegetables

SERVES 4 (65 Calories per serving)

This recipe proves that lettuce needn't be limited to use in salads.

4 lettuce hearts (crisp and tight)

1 teaspoon vegetable oil

4oz (120g) onion, thinly sliced

1 medium carrot, cut into matchstick-sized pieces

2oz (60g) boiled ham, cut into thin strips

8fl oz (240ml) chicken stock

½ bay leaf

¼ teaspoon pepper

1 teaspoon plain flour

1 teaspoon margarine, softened

Boil the lettuce hearts for 1 minute, plunge briefly into cold water, drain and set aside.

Heat the oil in a saucepan, add the onion and carrot and cook gently for 3–4 minutes until the vegetables soften. Reduce the heat to low and stir in the ham, stock and seasonings, cover and simmer gently for 15 minutes. Add the lettuce hearts and cook for a further 10 minutes.

In a small bowl mix the flour and margarine well together. Gradually add the mixture to the saucepan, stirring well after each addition until the margarine has dissolved and the flour been absorbed. Continue stirring over a low heat until the sauce thickens, about 5 minutes.

To serve, place the lettuce hearts on a warm serving dish and surround with the vegetable mixture, pour the sauce over the hearts and vegetables.

EXCHANGES PER SERVING: 1½ Vegetable
½ Fat
½ Protein
5 Calories Optional

Brioches (p 96)

Brioches

SERVES 12 (240 Calories per serving)

Enjoy these brioches for breakfast or remove the topknot and fill with a savoury stuffing for lunch.

1½ teaspoons oil

2 teaspoons dried yeast

5 tablespoons warm water

1 tablespoon caster sugar

1lb 2oz (540g) strong white bread flour

½ teaspoon salt

3oz (90g) or 6 tablespoons margarine

4 large eggs, beaten

2 teaspoons skimmed milk

Brush twelve deep bun tins or individual brioche tins and a sheet of clingfilm with the oil.

Mix the yeast and warm water together in a bowl, stir until the yeast dissolves. Mix in ½ teaspoon caster sugar and 3oz (90g) flour. Beat well to form a wet dough, cover with the greased clingfilm and leave in a warm place until it froths up like a sponge, about 30 minutes.

Reserve 2 tablespoons flour, sieve the remainder into a bowl with the rest of the sugar, stir in the salt and rub in the margarine. Mix in the yeast dough and sufficient beaten egg to make a firm, not sticky, dough. This will take nearly all the egg. Sprinkle a little of the reserved flour over the work surface and knead the dough until smooth and elastic, about 10 minutes, or use an electric mixer fitted with a dough hook and work for about 3 minutes. Transfer the dough to a clean bowl, cover with the greased clingfilm and leave to prove in a warm place until doubled in size, about 45–60 minutes. Using the rest of the reserved flour, sprinkle the work surface. Remove the dough from the bowl and knead for 1–2 minutes. Shape three-quarters of the dough into twelve balls, place each ball in a greased tin. Roll the remaining dough into twelve small balls, dampen one side and press damp side down onto the larger balls of dough. Cover with the greased clingfilm and leave in the warm until well risen or about doubled in size. Preheat the oven to 425°F, 220°C, Gas Mark 7. Brush the risen brioches with the remaining beaten egg mixed with the milk and bake in the preheated oven for 15 minutes until golden brown. Cool on a wire rack.

EXCHANGES PER SERVING: 1½ Fat
1½ Bread
30 Calories Optional

Pear Sorbet

EXCHANGES PER SERVING: 1 Fruit
10 Calories Optional

SERVES 4 (60 Calories per serving)

This delicious dessert is simple to make and leaves the palate refreshed.

4 medium pears, peeled, cored and sliced

1 tablespoon lemon juice

2 teaspoons golden syrup

ground ginger

sprigs of mint to garnish

Place the pear slices, lemon juice, golden syrup and a sprinkling of ground ginger in a blender or food processor. Process until smooth. Pour the puree into an 8 × 8 × 2-inch (20 × 20 × 5-cm) freezerproof container, cover with clingfilm and freeze until the edges of the mixture are firm, about 3 hours.

Scrape all the mixture into a large bowl and, using an electric whisk, whisk until smooth but not melted. Transfer to a suitable freezerproof container, cover and return to the freezer until firm.

To serve, scoop the sorbet into four serving glasses and garnish with sprigs of fresh mint.

Black Cherry Clafouti

SERVES 6 (175 Calories per serving)

This French fruit pudding is a classic. To ensure the batter is completely cooked, carefully insert a knife in the centre of the pudding. If the knife comes out clean it is cooked, if not return to the oven for a few more minutes.

1 teaspoon vegetable oil

12oz (360g) large dark sweet cherries, stoned

3oz (90g) skimmed milk powder, made up to 12fl oz (360ml) with cold water

3 eggs

1 teaspoon vanilla essence

large pinch ground cinnamon

large pinch salt

ground nutmeg

3oz (90g) self raising flour

Preheat the oven to 375°F, 190°C, Gas Mark 5. Brush a 9-inch (22.5-cm) pie plate with the oil and spread the cherries over the bottom.

Using an electric mixer, whisk together the milk, eggs, vanilla, cinnamon, salt and a sprinkling of nutmeg for about 1 minute. Sieve the flour and stir into the mixture until smooth. Pour the batter over the cherries and bake for 35–40 minutes. Serve warm.

EXCHANGES PER SERVING: ½ Fruit
½ Milk
½ Protein
½ Bread
10 Calories Optional

GERMANY

If you look at a German menu, you may be surprised to see that 'heaven and earth' is being served. In fact, 'Himmel und Erde' is what the Germans call the dish which combines two of their favourite foods: potatoes and apples.

A robust people, the Germans opt for substantial meals. Pork in some form is on almost every menu, often paired with sauerkraut. Sausages are immensely popular, onions appear in almost every dish, and sweet paprika and poppy seeds are basic seasonings. The Germans have a predilection for sweet and sour dishes like Rotkohl, red cabbage with vinegar and brown sugar, and apples are used in many savoury dishes.

One of the sweets we have chosen is based on apples, the Adventsbratapfel, but transformed with a tasty filling of oats and raisins. The other is a delicate pineapple mousse which will be very welcome at the end of a substantial meal, but both desserts are very popular with children and make great buffet additions.

To complete your germanic feast, choose some of the country's world-famous beer, or a glass of one of their light and fruity wines.

MENU

Birnensuppe

Pork Chops with Apples and Sauerkraut

Kartoffelsalat

Ananasmousse

coffee

white wine or beer

Birnen-suppe

EXCHANGES PER SERVING: 1½ Fruit
35 Calories Optional

SERVES 4 (125 Calories per serving)

Pear soup, flavoured with cinnamon and served chilled.

2oz (60g) raisins

4 tablespoons dry sherry

4 medium pears, peeled, cored and sliced

15fl oz (450ml) water

1–1½-inch (2.5–4-cm) cinnamon stick

crushed aniseed

4 teaspoons caster sugar

1 teaspoon lemon juice

4 lemon slices to garnish

Mix the raisins and sherry together in a small bowl, set aside.

Place the pears, water, cinnamon stick and a sprinkling of aniseed together in a saucepan, bring to the boil and cook until the pears are very soft, about 15 minutes. Leave the mixture to cool and remove the cinnamon stick. Pour the cool mixture into a blender and process until smooth, pour into a bowl and stir in the raisins and sherry, sugar and lemon juice. Cover and refrigerate until well chilled. Garnish with lemon slices before serving.

Pork Chops with Apples and Sauerkraut

SERVES 4 (260 Calories per serving)

In true German fashion, accompany this dish with a mug of chilled beer.

4 teaspoons margarine

2 medium apples, cored and sliced

1 onion, sliced

8 oz (240g) drained sauerkraut

6fl oz (180ml) chicken stock

1 tablespoon Dijon-style mustard

1 teaspoon caraway seeds

¼ teaspoon coarsely ground black pepper

4 × 6-oz (180-g) pork loin chops, about ½ inch (1cm) thick

parsley sprigs to garnish

Heat the margarine in a large frying pan over a high heat until hot and bubbling. Saute the apple and onion for 2–3 minutes until beginning to colour, remove from the frying pan and set aside. Add the sauerkraut, stir in the chicken stock, mustard and seasonings. Reduce the heat, cover and simmer, stirring occasionally for 8–10 minutes.

While the sauce is simmering, grill the pork chops for 4–5 minutes on each side. Add the chops and the reserved apple mixture to the pan and simmer until the apple slices are cooked through but still retain their shape, about 2 minutes. Place the chops on warm serving plates and surround with the sauerkraut mixture. Garnish with parsley sprigs.

EXCHANGES PER SERVING: 1 Fat
½ Fruit
1 Vegetable
4 Protein
5 Calories Optional

Top: Ananasmousse (p 112)
Centre: Birnensuppe (p 101)
Bottom: Pork Chops with Sauerkraut

Rotkohl

EXCHANGES PER SERVING: 2 Vegetable
½ Fat
30 Calories Optional

SERVES 12 (75 Calories per serving)

This is our version of red cabbage, a classic German dish.

3lb 8oz–4lb (1kg 680g–1kg 920g) head red cabbage, trimmed, cored and finely shredded

4fl oz (120ml) red wine vinegar

2 tablespoons vegetable oil

6oz (180g) onion, diced

3 medium tart apples, peeled, cored and thinly sliced

2 tablespoons brown sugar

2 teaspoons salt

2 bay leaves

½ teaspoon pepper

6 whole cloves

4 tablespoons dry red wine

Toss the red cabbage and vinegar in a bowl, set aside. Heat the oil in a large non-stick frying pan over a medium heat, add the onions and saute until translucent. Add the cabbage mixture and all the remaining ingredients except the wine, stir to combine. Reduce the heat to low, cover and steam for about 15 minutes or until the cabbage is cooked to taste. Stir in the wine and cook uncovered for about 5 minutes. Remove the bay leaves and cloves before serving.

Kalbsleber auf Berliner Art

SERVES 2 (315 Calories per serving)

Apple and onion rings dress up this Berlin-style liver dish.

4 teaspoons low-fat spread

2oz (60g) onion, thinly sliced and separated into rings

1 medium apple, cored, peeled and cut into ¼-inch (5-mm) thick rings

1 tablespoon plain flour

¼ teaspoon salt

large pinch pepper

2 × 5-oz (150-g) slices calf or lamb's liver

Heat 1 teaspoon low-fat spread in a large frying pan until hot and bubbling. Add the onion rings and saute until lightly browned. Using a slotted spoon, transfer the onion to a warm plate and keep warm. Add a second teaspoon of low-fat spread to the frying pan and heat until bubbling. Add the apple rings and saute until golden on both sides. Transfer to the plate with the onion. Season the flour with the salt and pepper. Turn the liver slices in the seasoned flour.

Heat the remaining low-fat spread in the frying pan. When hot and bubbling add the liver and cook, turning once. Do not overcook or the liver will become tough. Transfer the liver to a warm serving plate and top with the onion and apple rings.

EXCHANGES PER SERVING: 1 Fat
½ Vegetable
½ Fruit
4 Protein
15 Calories Optional

Konigsberger Klopse

SERVES 4 (365 Calories per serving)

Meatballs Konigsberg-style, a blend of beef and pork given added interest by the flavour of capers.

1oz (30g) fresh white breadcrumbs
2 tablespoons water
12oz (360g) minced beef
6oz (180g) minced pork
2oz (60g) onion, chopped
2 eggs
1½ teaspoons caper juice (from bottled capers)
1 teaspoon lemon juice
½ teaspoon salt
¼ teaspoon pepper
¼ teaspoon grated lemon zest
1 pint 4fl oz (720ml) chicken stock
4 teaspoons margarine
1oz (30g) plain flour
4 tablespoons dry white wine
2 teaspoons chopped or small drained capers

Soak the breadcrumbs in the water. Mix together the beef, pork, half the onion, 1 egg, the caper juice, lemon juice, salt, pepper and lemon peel. Mix in the soaked breadcrumbs. Shape the mixture into twelve even-sized meatballs and place them on the rack of a grill pan. Grill the meatballs until browned and cooked through. Bring the chicken stock to the boil in a large saucepan, add the meatballs and simmer for 12 minutes or until cooked according to taste. Transfer the meatballs to a deep serving dish and keep warm, reserve the cooking liquid.

Heat the margarine until hot and bubbling in a clean saucepan. Add the remaining onion and saute until softened. Stir in the flour and cook, stirring constantly, for 2–3 minutes. Gradually blend in the wine and the reserved cooking liquid. Simmer gently, stirring from time to time, until the sauce is thick and smooth. Stir in the capers and remove from the heat. Beat the remaining egg in a small bowl, stir about 4fl oz (120ml) sauce into the egg and gradually pour the egg mixture into the remaining sauce, stirring rapidly to prevent lumping. Cook, stirring constantly, until the sauce is heated through but do not allow to boil. Pour the sauce over the warm meatballs and serve immediately.

EXCHANGES PER SERVING: ½ Bread
4 Protein
1 Fat
15 Calories Optional

Himmel und Erde (p 108)

tragstücke

Himmel und Erde

SERVES 4 (170 Calories per serving)

This delicious mixture of potatoes, apple and ham is a typically German side dish. The name means 'heaven and earth'.

12oz (360g) peeled potatoes, cut into cubes

4fl oz (120ml) boiling water

½ teaspoon salt

2 medium apples, peeled, quartered, cored and sliced

4 teaspoons low-fat spread

3oz (90g) onion, diced

4oz (120g) boiled ham, cut into cubes

sprig of parsley to garnish

Place the potatoes, boiling water and salt in a saucepan and boil until the potatoes are almost tender, about 15 minutes. Stir in the apple and cook over a low heat until the apples are tender-crisp, stirring occasionally.

While the potatoes are cooking, heat the low-fat spread in a small saucepan. Add the onion and saute until softened, stir in the ham and continue cooking until the onion turns golden brown.

Mash the potato until blended but still lumpy, stir in some of the ham and onion mixture, spoon into a warm serving dish. Top with the remaining onion and ham, garnish with parsley and serve.

EXCHANGES PER SERVING:	1 Bread
	½ Fruit
	½ Fat
	½ Vegetable
	1 Protein

Sauerkraut Salad

SERVES 4 (90 Calories per serving)

A cold version of a favourite combination: sauerkraut, apples and onion.

12oz (360g) drained sauerkraut

2 medium Golden Delicious apples, peeled, cored and grated

4oz (120g) red onion, diced

4 teaspoons vegetable oil

pepper to taste

Combine all the ingredients in a mixing bowl, cover and refrigerate for at least 2 hours. Toss well before serving.

EXCHANGES PER SERVING: 1½ Vegetable
½ Fruit
1 Fat

Kartoffel-salat

EXCHANGES PER SERVING:	1 Bread
	1 Fat
	1½ Vegetable

SERVES 4 (135 Calories per serving)

This German potato salad can either be made with warm, freshly boiled potatoes or chilled. If you take it on a picnic it is advisable to carry the cucumber and beetroot separately.

12oz (360g) cooked potatoes, thinly sliced
salt and pepper
½ teaspoon chopped parsley
½ teaspoon chopped chives
4 tablespoons chicken stock
4 teaspoons vegetable oil
2 teaspoons wine vinegar
12oz (360g) cucumber, sliced
4oz (120g) cooked beetroot, sliced

Layer the slices of potato in a salad bowl. Season each layer with salt and pepper to taste and sprinkle with a few chopped parsley leaves and chives. Whisk the chicken stock, oil and vinegar together in a small bowl or shake in a screw top jar to mix well. Pour the dressing over the salad and mix lightly. Serve warm with the cucumber and beetroot or cover and refrigerate before serving.

Advents-bratapfel

SERVES 2 (215 Calories per serving)

EXCHANGES PER SERVING:	1½ Fruit
	1 Fat
	½ Bread
	30 Calories Optional

This delicious recipe can be made with tart dessert apples or cooking apples, whichever you prefer.

1oz (30g) raisins

2 teaspoons white wine

few drops of rum flavouring

2 teaspoons margarine

1oz (30g) rolled oats

1 tablespoon desiccated coconut

1 teaspoon sugar

2 medium apples

Soak the raisins in the wine and a few drops of rum flavouring, overnight or for at least 2 hours. Preheat the oven at 375°F, 190°C, Gas Mark 5. Melt the margarine in a non-stick frying pan, add the rolled oats, desiccated coconut and sugar and saute until golden brown. Mix the raisins into the rolled oat mixture. Core the apples and fill with the mixture. Score round the middle of each apple and place in an ovenproof dish. Bake in the preheated oven for about 30 minutes until the apples are cooked.

Ananas-mousse

SERVES 4 (75 Calories per serving)

This pineapple mousse is simple to make and looks attractive decorated with the halved strawberries and sliced kiwi fruit.

8oz (240g) well drained, canned, unsweetened pineapple and 2 tablespoons juice

3 tablespoons lemon juice

pinch of salt

4 teaspoons gelatine

3 tablespoons water

5fl oz (150ml) skimmed milk

few drops vanilla flavouring

artificial sweetener to taste

TO DECORATE:

5oz (150g) strawberries, halved

1 medium kiwi fruit, peeled and sliced

Place the pineapple, its juice, the lemon juice and a pinch of salt in a blender and process until smooth. Mix the gelatine and water together in a small bowl and stand the bowl in a pan of simmering water until the gelatine has dissolved. Mix the milk and vanilla essence together, slowly stir in the dissolved gelatine. Whisk the mixture 4–5 minutes until very frothy. Stir in the pineapple puree and sweeten to taste. Spoon the mousse into serving glasses and chill until firm. Decorate with the strawberries and kiwi fruit before serving.

EXCHANGES PER SERVING: 1 Fruit
15 Calories Optional

GREECE

'The cuisine which inspired a poet'. The Athenian poet Archestratus is thought to have written the world's first known cookbook nearly 2,400 years ago.

The countryside of Europe's oldest civilisation blooms with the fragrant lemons so widely used for flavouring. As in ancient times, the landscape is dotted with olive trees, source of the world-famous olives and of the oil that is such an integral part of Greek cooking. The culinary term 'a la Grecque' usually means prepared with olive oil.

Feta, the national cheese, shows up in an array of dishes. We have included it in recipes for prawns, fish and beef. Seafood is another speciality of this land mostly surrounded by water: the Greeks are said to be the first to have discovered that oysters were edible. Although lamb is usually associated with Greek cuisine, beef is becoming increasingly popular. We give you the recipe for a classic beef and savoury custard casserole – Sfougato – from the island of Rhodes.

Dolmades, the well-known stuffed vine leaves, are a popular dish in Greece and all over the Balkan countries, with some variations in the filling. Our suggestion includes rice and can be used as a starter or as a vegetable dish.

Honey Twists make use of one of the ingredients Greece is most famous for. Since time immemorial, Mount Hymettus is thought to have produced the world's best honey. Whatever your choice, it would be a pity to keep these ideas for use only on summer days. Why not brighten up a grey winter day with a colourful and tasty selection from this sunny land?

MENU

Greek Marinated Vegetable Salad

Prawns with Tomatoes and Feta Cheese

rice and courgettes

Honeyed Greek Salad

coffee

white wine

Greek Marinated Vegetable Salad

SERVES 4 (60 Calories per serving)

Aubergine, red pepper, artichoke hearts and mushrooms in a tasty herbed marinade.

1 × 6-oz (180-g) aubergine

1 medium red pepper

8oz (240g) drained, canned artichoke hearts

1 teaspoon olive oil

4oz (120g) small mushroom caps, cut into quarters

FOR THE DRESSING:

1 tablespoon olive oil

1 tablespoon lemon juice

2 garlic cloves, crushed

1 teaspoon oregano

1 teaspoon red wine vinegar

¼ teaspoon marjoram

¼ teaspoon thyme

¼ teaspoon basil

¼ teaspoon pepper

Place the whole aubergine and pepper under a hot grill and cook for about 3 minutes, turning frequently until the skin blisters and is charred. Plunge the hot vegetables into a bowl of cold water. When cool enough to handle, peel away as much skin as possible from the pepper, remove and discard the seeds and cut into thin strips. Peel and dice the aubergine and place in a bowl with the pepper strips and artichoke hearts, set aside.

Heat the teaspoon of olive oil and saute the mushrooms in it for 2–3 minutes. When they are cooked, add them to the rest of the vegetables in the bowl.

To make the dressing: Place all the dressing ingredients in a small bowl and whisk together or shake in a screw top jar to mix well. Pour the dressing over the vegetables and toss to coat, cover with clingfilm and marinade for at least 30 minutes.

EXCHANGES PER SERVING: 1½ Vegetable
1 Fat

Dolmades with Lemon Sauce

SERVES 4 (155 Calories per serving, excluding Lemon Sauce** or **220 Calories per serving, including Lemon Sauce)

Stuffed vine leaves, a classic Greek appetiser.

2 teaspoons olive oil

3oz (90g) onion, finely chopped

2 garlic cloves, finely chopped

2oz (60g) long grain rice

1 pint (600ml) water

2 tomatoes, peeled and finely chopped

4oz (120g) sultanas

2 tablespoons chopped parsley

1 teaspoon salt

¼ teaspoon ground cinnamon

pepper

20 vacuum-packed vine leaves, well rinsed

2 lemons, cut in thin wedges

Lemon Sauce (see page 117)

Heat 1 teaspoon oil in a medium-sized frying pan. Add the onion and garlic and saute until the onion is golden, stir in the rice and cook for a further minute. Add 12fl oz (360ml) water, the tomatoes, sultanas, parsley, salt, cinnamon and a sprinkling of pepper. Stir well and bring to the boil. Reduce the heat, cover and simmer until the rice is tender, about 15 minutes.

Spoon an equal amount of the rice mixture onto the stem end of each vine leaf, fold the stem over, then fold the sides neatly over the filling. Roll each leaf up Swiss roll fashion. Transfer the leaves, seam-side down, to the same frying pan and pour in the remaining water. Brush the remaining oil over the base of a plate and rest oiled side down on top of the vine leaves. Weigh the plate down and cook over a high heat until the water comes to the boil. Reduce the heat and simmer for 15–20 minutes. Serve the stuffed vine leaves with lemon wedges and Lemon Sauce.

EXCHANGES PER SERVING (not including Lemon Sauce): ½ Fat
2 Vegetable
½ Bread
1 Fruit

Lemon Sauce

SERVES 4 (65 Calories per serving)

Serve this sauce with the dolmades on page 116.

2 eggs

1 tablespoon lemon juice

2 teaspoons margarine

½ teaspoon salt

paprika

Whisk the eggs and lemon juice together in a small heavy-based saucepan. Place over a very low heat and, whisking all the time, add 1 teaspoon margarine. When the margarine has melted, whisk in the remaining teaspoon margarine and continue whisking constantly until the sauce thickens. Do not overcook. Remove from the heat and season with salt and pepper. Use immediately.

EXCHANGES PER SERVING: ½ Protein
½ Fat

Greek-Style Vegetables

SERVES 4 (135 Calories per serving)

A melange of vegetables with a cheese topping.

12oz (360g) tomatoes, thinly sliced

9oz (270g) aubergine, cut in cubes

3oz (90g) spinach, chopped

3oz (90g) celery, diced

3oz (90g) onions, sliced

½ red pepper, seeded and sliced

½ green pepper, seeded and sliced

3 tablespoons lemon juice

4 teaspoons chopped dill

4 teaspoons olive oil

2 garlic cloves, finely chopped

¼ teaspoon pepper

4oz (120g) feta cheese, crumbled

sprig of dill to garnish

Preheat the oven to 400°F, 200°C, Gas Mark 6.

Arrange half the tomato slices in the bottom of a non-stick casserole dish. Mix the remaining tomatoes with the rest of the ingredients, except the cheese, in a large bowl. Toss well to combine. Spoon the vegetable mixture over the tomato slices, cover and bake in the preheated oven for 35–40 minutes until the vegetables are tender-crisp. Sprinkle the feta cheese over the vegetables and bake uncovered for a further 5–10 minutes. Garnish with a sprig of dill.

EXCHANGES PER SERVING: 3 Vegetable
1 Protein

Top: Greek-Style Vegetables
Bottom: Prawns with Tomatoes and Feta Cheese (p 120)

Prawns with Tomatoes and Feta Cheese

SERVES 4 (220 Calories per serving)

This recipe makes a colourful main course, suitable for a dinner party.

4 teaspoons olive oil
7oz (210g) aubergine, chopped
1 small yellow pepper, seeded and chopped
4 spring onions, sliced
3–4 garlic cloves, finely chopped
1lb (480g) tomatoes, peeled and chopped
4 tablespoons dry white wine
4 tablespoons water
2 tablespoons chopped parsley
4 teaspoons grated lemon zest
1 teaspoon oregano
½ teaspoon pepper
14oz (420g) large peeled prawns (leave a few unpeeled for garnish if desired)
2oz (60g) feta cheese, crumbled

Heat the oil in a large frying pan over a high heat. Add the aubergine and saute, stirring all the time, until browned on all sides. Add the pepper, spring onions and garlic and saute for a further 1 minute. Stir in the remaining ingredients, except the prawns and cheese. Reduce the heat to medium and cook, stirring occasionally, for 3–5 minutes. Stir in the prawns and cook until the prawns have heated through and the cheese is beginning to melt. Do not overcook. Serve immediately.

EXCHANGES PER SERVING: 1 Fat
2 Vegetable
4 Protein
15 Calories Optional

Stuffed Plaice Athenian

SERVES 2 (185 Calories per serving)

Spinach and feta cheese combine well in the filling of this typically Greek dish.

7–8oz (210–240g) well-drained cooked chopped spinach

2oz (60g) feta cheese, crumbled

4 teaspoons lemon juice

¼ teaspoon dillweed

¼ teaspoon pepper

2 × 4-oz (120-g) plaice fillets

4 tablespoons water

2 tablespoons dry white wine

1 tablespoon chopped parsley

large pinch paprika

Preheat the oven to 375°F, 190°C, Gas Mark 5.

Mix together the spinach, cheese, 2 teaspoons lemon juice, the dill and pepper. Lay out the plaice fillets and spoon half of the spinach mixture along the centre of each fillet. Roll the fish lengthwise to enclose the filling and place seam-side down in an 8 × 8 × 2-inch (20 × 20 × 5-cm) ovenproof dish.

Mix together the water, wine, parsley, paprika and remaining lemon juice, pour over the fillets and bake in the preheated oven for 15–20 minutes until the fish flakes when tested with a fork.

EXCHANGES PER SERVING: 1½ Vegetable
4 Protein
15 Calories Optional

Sfougato

SERVES 4 (355 Calories per serving)

Courgettes and onions add flavour and texture to this delicious Greek beef custard.

2 teaspoons olive oil

2 teaspoons margarine

6oz (180g) onion, diced

4oz (120g) courgettes, grated

10oz (300g) cooked minced beef, crumbled

16fl oz (480ml) skimmed milk

6 eggs, beaten

4 teaspoons chopped parsley

½ teaspoon salt

pepper

tomato slices, sprigs of chervil or parsley, to garnish

Preheat the oven to 350°F, 180°C, Gas Mark 4. Use a little of the oil to grease a non-stick casserole dish. Heat the remaining oil and margarine in a medium-sized frying pan until hot and bubbling. Add the onion and courgette and saute 3–4 minutes, stirring occasionally, until the onion is soft. Transfer the vegetables to a bowl and add the minced beef, milk, eggs, parsley, salt and a sprinkling of pepper. Stir well to combine, then pour into the greased casserole dish and bake in the centre of the preheated oven for 40–50 minutes until firm. Garnish with tomato and herbs.

EXCHANGES PER SERVING: 1 Fat
1 Vegetable
4 Protein
¼ Milk
15 Calories Optional

Sfougato

Lemon-Chicken Oregano

SERVES 2 (230 Calories per serving)

In Greece, lemon is highly favoured as a seasoning and is frequently used with poultry as well as fish.

1½ teaspoons margarine

1 tablespoon lemon juice

1½ teaspoons olive oil

1 small garlic clove, crushed

½ teaspoon oregano

¼ teaspoon salt

¼ teaspoon pepper

2 × 5-oz (150-g) skinned and boned chicken breasts

TO GARNISH:

2 lemon slices

1 teaspoon chopped parsley

Melt the margarine in a small saucepan, add the lemon juice, oil, garlic, oregano, salt and pepper and bring to the boil. Reduce the heat to low and simmer for 1 minute. Transfer to a mixing bowl and allow to cool completely before adding the chicken. Turn the chicken in the marinade, cover and refrigerate for at least 1 hour or, if possible, overnight.

Transfer the chicken to a shallow baking dish large enough to hold the chicken in a single layer. Brush half the marinade over the chicken and grill for 4 minutes. Turn the chicken over and brush with the remaining marinade, return to the grill for a further 4 minutes or until browned and cooked.

To serve, transfer the chicken to a warm serving plate, pour over any pan juices and garnish with the lemon slices and chopped parsley.

EXCHANGES PER SERVING: 1½ Fat
4 Protein

Honeyed Greek Salad

EXCHANGES PER SERVING: 2 Fruit
15 Calories Optional

SERVES 4 (95 Calories per serving)

The grape juice, honey and rosewater give this fruit salad an extra special flavour.

8fl oz (240ml) white grape juice

1 tablespoon honey

1 teaspoon rose water

4 medium apricots, stoned and cut into thin wedges

1 medium peach or nectarine, stoned and cut into thin wedges

2 dates, stoned and cut into long strips

2 large figs, peeled and thinly sliced

3oz (90g) grapes, halved and seeded

Place the grape juice and honey in a small saucepan and heat gently until the honey has dissolved. Remove from the heat, stir in the rose water and leave until cold. Mix all the prepared fruits together in a serving bowl, pour over the cool syrup and leave to marinade for at least an hour before serving.

Greek Honey Twists

SERVES 6 (280 Calories per serving)

A dessert that does honour to the celebrated Greek honey.

3 eggs, beaten

9oz (270g) plain flour

½ teaspoon baking powder

¼ teaspoon salt

2 tablespoons vegetable oil

2 tablespoons honey

2 tablespoons caster sugar

¼ teaspoon ground cinnamon

Measure out and reserve 2 tablespoons of the beaten eggs. Sieve the flour, baking powder and salt into a mixing bowl, add the remaining egg, and stir in the oil. Turn out onto a flat surface and knead well until smooth and elastic, 8–10 minutes. Cover the dough and leave to rest for 10–15 minutes.

Preheat the oven to 375°F, 190°C, Gas Mark 5. Roll out the dough between two sheets of baking parchment to a thickness of about ¼ inch (3mm) to form an 18 × 8-inch (46 × 20-cm) rectangle. Cut into eighteen 8 × 1-inch (20 × 5-cm) strips. Twist each strip of dough and place on a non-stick baking sheet or a baking sheet lined with baking parchment. Brush each twist with an equal amount of the reserved egg and bake in the preheated oven until golden, 8–10 minutes. Transfer to a wire rack to cool.

In a small saucepan, heat the honey, sugar and cinnamon over a medium heat, stirring all the time until the sugar dissolves and the mixture is smooth and syrupy, 3–4 minutes. Transfer the twists to a serving plate and trickle the syrup over them, allowing about ¾ teaspoon per twist.

EXCHANGES PER SERVING: ½ Protein
1½ Bread
1 Fat
40 Calories Optional

INDIA

If it hadn't been for India's spices, the history of the world would have been very different, for it was in search of those precious seasonings that Columbus set sail.

They are put to their most renowned use in Kari, or, as we call it, curry. Kari isn't the familiar commercially prepared powder, but a combination of herbs and spices, with or without a sauce. The mixes differ from one family to another, and the secret formulas are handed down like heirlooms. Among the most common ingredients are cardamom, coriander, turmeric, cumin and ginger. Curry is not necessarily fiery; the 'temperature' can be adjusted from hot to mild.

The traditional accompaniment for all curry dishes is chutney, a vegetable or fruit relish. Its ingredients also vary, but in our adaptation we use oranges and dates.

India's eating habits are determined as much by region as by religion: Moslems don't eat pork, the vast Hindu population is vegetarian, and for most sects cattle are sacred. Because of these factors, as well as of economy, vegetables are the core of Indian menus. They appear in curries like our Mixed Vegetables or in raitas, salad-like combinations in a cooling yogurt base.

In Tandoori Chicken, a highly regarded dish, the poultry is marinated in various spices and takes on a reddish colouring. The Indians have also provided us with a soup that has become world famous: the spicy Mulligatawny, which is aptly named since it combines pepper (molegoo) with water (tunee).

For a genuine Indian meal, serve all the courses at the same time and let our dishes put spice into your life!

MENU

Curried Prawns with Saffron Rice

Radish Raita

Orange-Date Chutney

Indian 'Fried' Bread

fresh mango

tea

Mulliga-tawny Soup

SERVES 4 (265 Calories per serving)

From exotic India, a delicious version of chicken soup.

1 tablespoon margarine

1 teaspoon vegetable oil

1½lbs (720g) chicken portions

12oz (360g) onions, chopped

1 medium green pepper, seeded and cut into thin strips

4oz (120g) celery, chopped

5oz (150g) carrot, chopped

1 pint 6fl oz (780ml) water

2 medium cooking apples, peeled, cored and chopped

8fl oz (240ml) apple juice

1½ teaspoons salt

1 teaspoon desiccated coconut

1 teaspoon curry powder

1 teaspoon lemon juice

large pinch ground cloves

large pinch ground mace

large pinch ground coriander

paprika

Heat the margarine and oil in a large saucepan until the margarine is hot and bubbling. Saute the chicken portions until brown on all sides. Transfer the chicken to a plate and set aside. Stir the vegetables into the same saucepan and saute until the onions are translucent. Return the chicken to the saucepan and stir in all the remaining ingredients. Bring to the boil, reduce the heat, cover and simmer gently for about 30 minutes until the chicken is cooked and the vegetables tender. Remove the chicken from the saucepan and allow to cool, then remove the meat from the chicken pieces and shred or chop it into small portions. Return the meat to the saucepan, reheat and serve piping hot.

EXCHANGES PER SERVING: 1 Fat
4 Protein
2 Vegetable
1 Fruit
5 Calories Optional

Curried Prawns with Saffron Rice

SERVES 4 (410 Calories per serving)

The colourful garnish of uncooked vegetables makes this a very special dish.

FOR THE RICE:

8oz (240g) long grain rice

8fl oz (240ml) water

1 teaspoon salt

¼ teaspoon ground saffron

FOR THE CURRIED PRAWNS:

1 tablespoon margarine

4oz (120g) onions, thinly sliced

1 medium apple, cored and chopped

1oz (30g) sultanas

2 tablespoons lime or lemon juice

1 teaspoon curry powder

1 teaspoon salt

1 bay leaf

1 small garlic clove, finely chopped

½ teaspoon ground ginger

½ teaspoon ground cardamom

¼ teaspoon grated lemon zest

1lb (480g) large peeled prawns

TO GARNISH:

4oz (120g) green and red pepper, seeded and cut into matchstick-sized pieces

4oz (120g) tomatoes, diced

1oz (30g) cucumber, sliced

2oz (60g) onion, chopped

To prepare the rice: Stir all the rice ingredients together in a saucepan. Bring to the boil, reduce the heat, cover and simmer until the rice has absorbed the liquid and is tender, 15–20 minutes.

To prepare the curried prawns: While the rice is cooking, heat the margarine in a large non-stick frying pan. When hot and bubbling, add the onions and saute until golden. Stir in the remaining ingredients except the prawns and garnish. Reduce the heat and simmer until the apple is soft, about 5 minutes. Increase the heat, add the prawns and stir over the high heat until the prawns are heated through.

To serve, spoon the rice onto a warmed serving plate, arrange the prawn mixture next to the rice and arrange the garnishes decoratively over and round the curry.

EXCHANGES PER SERVING: 2 Bread
¾ Fat
1½ Vegetable
½ Fruit
4 Protein

Top: Naan Bread (p 132)
Bottom: Curried Prawns with Saffron Rice

Naan Bread

SERVES 12 (155 Calories per serving)

In India these oval breads are sprinkled with onion seeds; we have substituted poppy or sesame seeds. Traditionally they are served with Tandoori Chicken (see page 138).

1 tablespoon dried yeast

4fl oz (120ml) warm water

1 teaspoon caster sugar

12oz (360g) strong white bread flour

¼ teaspoon vegetable oil

½ teaspoon salt

4 tablespoons margarine, melted

2fl oz (60ml) or 4 tablespoons low-fat natural yogurt

1 egg, beaten

1 tablespoon poppy or sesame seeds

Sprinkle the yeast into 4 tablespoons warm water and stir until dissolved. Mix in the sugar and 2oz (60g) flour, beat well. Grease a sheet of clingfilm with the oil, cover the yeast mixture and leave in a warm place until it froths up like a sponge, about 15 minutes.

Reserve 2 tablespoons flour, sieve the remainder with the salt into a bowl. Mix in the frothy yeast mixture, 3 tablespoons margarine, the yogurt, egg and sufficient water to form a slightly sticky dough. Mix for 4–5 minutes. Cover the bowl with the greased clingfilm and leave in the warm until the dough has doubled in size, 35–45 minutes.

Preheat the oven to 425°F, 210°C, Gas Mark 7. Sprinkle the work surface with the reserved flour. Turn the dough out onto the floured surface, divide into 12 equal-sized pieces. Using floured hands, pat the pieces of dough into ovals 4–5 inches (10–12.5cm) in diameter. Arrange the ovals on non-stick baking sheets and brush with the remaining melted margarine, sprinkle with the poppy or sesame seeds and bake in the preheated oven for 10–12 minutes until puffed up and lightly browned.

EXCHANGES PER SERVING: 1 Bread
1 Fat
20 Calories Optional

Indian 'Fried' Bread

SERVES 4 (150 Calories per serving)

This slightly puffed bread is typical of the Indian cuisine. Add the water slowly as different flours require different amounts of liquid to make the dough.

4oz (120g) wholewheat or plain white flour

½ teaspoon salt

approximately 5 tablespoons water

4 teaspoons vegetable oil

1 tablespoon flour for rolling out dough

Mix together the flour and salt. Using the slow speed of an electric mixer, gradually add the water until the mixture resembles coarse meal. Form the dough into a ball and knead for about 5 minutes on a dry surface. Cover with a damp cloth or clingfilm and leave to rest for 20 minutes. Use extra tablespoon flour to flour board and sprinkle on dough before rolling. Divide the dough into four equal pieces and roll each piece to form a circle as thin as possible. Heat 1 teaspoon oil in an 8–9-inch (20–23-cm) non-stick frying pan. Cook one piece of dough at a time until the dough is puffed up. Turn the dough frequently while it is cooking, 2–3 minutes. When puffed up and golden, transfer the bread to a plate and keep warm in an oven while cooking the remaining dough using the same procedure. Serve hot.

EXCHANGES PER SERVING: 1 Bread
1 Fat
10 Calories Optional

Orange-Date Chutney

SERVES 12 (60 Calories per serving)

No Indian meal is complete without this wonderful chutney. Properly refrigerated, this spicy relish will keep for months.

3 oranges

6oz (180g) onions, chopped

10 fresh or dried dates, stoned

4oz (120g) raisins

1 small garlic clove

4fl oz (120ml) distilled vinegar

2 tablespoons dark brown sugar

1 teaspoon salt

½ teaspoon ground cinnamon

½ teaspoon grated ginger root

¼ teaspoon chilli powder

¼ teaspoon ground nutmeg

Peel the zest from the oranges using a potato peeler. Place the zest in the bowl of a food processor. Remove all the remaining white pith and divide the orange into segments, removing all the membranes and catching any of the juice. Discard the pith and membranes and place the orange flesh and juice in the food processor with the onion, dates, raisins and garlic. Using the on-off motion, process the mixture until it is finely ground but not pureed. Bring the remaining ingredients to the boil in a saucepan. Stir in the fruit mixture and return to the boil. Cook for 3–5 minutes stirring constantly. Reduce the heat and simmer gently, stirring from time to time until most of the liquid has evaporated, 30–40 minutes. Remove from the heat and leave to cool. Transfer to a suitable container, cover and store in the refrigerator until ready to use.

EXCHANGES PER SERVING: 1 Fruit
½ Vegetable
10 Calories Optional

Mixed Vegetable Curry

SERVES 4 (185 Calories per serving)

If you enjoy hot and spicy food, this Pakistani speciality is for you. The rice helps to cool it down just a bit!

1–2 small green chillies, seeded and finely chopped

2 small garlic cloves, finely chopped

large pinch ground cumin

large pinch ground coriander

large pinch ground turmeric

4 teaspoons olive or vegetable oil

6oz (180g) potatoes, diced

6oz (180g) onions, chopped

5oz (150g) carrots, diced

1 green pepper, seeded and diced

1 red pepper, seeded and diced

3 medium tomatoes, peeled and chopped

1 teaspoon salt

6–8fl oz (180–240ml) water

12oz (360g) cooked long grain rice

parsley or coriander sprigs to garnish

Using a pestle and mortar, or a small bowl and the back of a spoon, crush the chillies, garlic, cumin, coriander and turmeric together to form a paste. Heat the oil in a large frying pan, add the chilli mixture and saute, stirring all the time, for 2–3 minutes. Add the potatoes, onions, carrots, peppers, tomatoes and salt, stirring to combine. Pour in just sufficient water to cover the vegetables and bring to the boil. Reduce the heat and simmer until the vegetables are just tender, 15–20 minutes.

To serve, mound the vegetable mixture on a warm serving plate, pile the rice beside the vegetables and decorate with parsley or coriander.

EXCHANGES PER SERVING: 1 Fat
1½ Bread
2 Vegetable

Radish Raita

SERVES 4 (25 Calories per serving)

A raita is a mixture of yogurt and vegetables and may be served as a salad or an appetiser. Indian raitas are cooling accompaniments to curries.

8oz (240g) radishes, grated

1 teaspoon salt

8 tablespoons low-fat natural yogurt

ground cumin

paprika

mint sprigs to garnish

Place the radishes in a colander and sprinkle with the salt, leave to drain 30–40 minutes. Squeeze out any excess water and transfer the radishes to a bowl. Stir in the yogurt and a sprinkling of cumin. Dust with a little paprika and garnish with sprigs of mint.

EXCHANGES PER SERVING: 1 Vegetable
20 Calories Optional

Tandoori Chicken

SERVES 4 (335 Calories per serving)

If you wish to make this recipe you should plan it well in advance as the chicken must be allowed to marinate for at least 8 hours to make sure that the flavourings are absorbed.

6oz (180g) onions, chopped

4fl oz (120ml) low-fat natural yogurt

4 tablespoons lemon or lime juice

1 tablespoon seeded, chopped green chilli

3–6 small garlic cloves, chopped

1 teaspoon peeled and finely chopped ginger root

large pinch ground turmeric

large pinch ground cinnamon

large pinch ground cardamom

large pinch ground cloves

large pinch ground allspice

salt

3lb (1kg 440g) chicken, cut into quarters and skinned

2 teaspoons olive or vegetable oil

1 tablespoon chopped coriander leaves to garnish

Place the onion, yogurt, lemon or lime juice, chilli, garlic and seasonings in a blender and process until smooth, scraping down the sides of the container as necessary. Using a sharp knife, make cuts in the chicken but do not pierce to the bone. Place the chicken in a mixing bowl and rub the yogurt mixture all over the chicken to coat. Cover the bowl with clingfilm and leave for at least 8 hours in the refrigerator. Preheat the oven to 475°F, 250°C, Gas Mark 9. Transfer the chicken to the rack in a roasting tin and brush with any remaining marinade. Roast for 20 minutes. Brush the chicken pieces with oil and continue cooking for about 10 minutes until the juices from the chicken run clear. Transfer the chicken to a serving dish, pour over the pan juices and garnish with the chopped coriander.

EXCHANGES PER SERVING:	4 Protein
	½ Fat
	20 Calories Optional

Payasam

SERVES 4 (245 Calories per serving)

EXCHANGES PER SERVING: 1½ Fat
1 Bread
¼ Milk
½ Fruit
15 Calories Optional

Saffron noodles and sultanas combine to make a delicious Indian dessert that can be served hot or lukewarm.

2 tablespoons margarine

4oz (120g) uncooked vermicelli, broken into 1-inch (2.5-cm) lengths

5fl oz (150ml) boiling water

10fl oz (300ml) skimmed milk

1 tablespoon granulated sugar

powdered saffron

2oz (60g) sultanas

large pinch ground cardamom

Heat the margarine in a frying pan over a medium heat until hot and bubbling. Add the vermicelli and saute, stirring all the time, until lightly browned. Reduce the heat to low and pour in the boiling water, simmer gently until the vermicelli is tender, about 5 minutes. Stir in the milk, sugar and a sprinkling of saffron and cook, stirring occasionally, for a further 5 minutes. Remove from the heat and stir in the sultanas and cardamom.

Gajar Halva

SERVES 2 (155 Calories per serving)

EXCHANGES PER SERVING: 1 Vegetable
½ Fruit
1 Fat
30 Calories Optional

This sweet dish from Pakistan may be served hot or chilled.

4fl oz (120ml) skimmed milk
4oz (120g) carrots, grated
1oz (30g) raisins
1½ teaspoons honey
2 teaspoons margarine
large pinch ground cardamom
pinch ground saffron
4 teaspoons desiccated coconut

Bring the milk to the boil in a heavy-based, small non-stick saucepan. Reduce the heat to low and stir in the carrots, raisins and honey. Cook, stirring occasionally, until the mixture becomes thick, 30–40 minutes. Stir in the remaining ingredients except the coconut and stir constantly until the margarine has melted. Transfer the mixture to a food processor or blender and process until smooth. Spoon into a serving dish and smooth the surface with a spatula, sprinkle with the desiccated coconut. Cover with clingfilm and refrigerate until chilled.

ITALY

When a strange red fruit reached Europe from the New World in the sixteenth century, botanists classified this so-called love apple as poisonous. Fortunately it was re-evaluated, and Italians have been in love with the tomato ever since.

Along with garlic and olive oil, tomatoes are basic to Italian cookery. But 'Italian' means different things, depending on where the dishes are cooked. In the northern regions, garlic is used more sparingly than in the south; butter, rather than oil, dominates the cooking, and rice dishes are preferred to pasta.

Southern Italy's love of pasta has long been recognised. Available in dozens of shapes and sizes, some pastas are eaten with sauces, others encase various stuffings, and some enrich soups like our Minestra di Pasta e Ceci. Pasta dishes frequently take on new colouring – as in our Linguine Verdi, 'painted' by spinach.

Served 'before the pasta', Italian antipasti, or hors d'oeuvres, customarily include anchovies. We've incorporated this fish into Italian Sour Dip from the Piedmont region.

Italian cooks use seasonings freely, not only garlic but herbs like oregano and the basil that's indispensable in tomato dishes. Cheese is also an essential ingredient, used in a variety of dishes from veal to dumplings, as in our Veal Valdostana.

Desserts are a prime pleasure for the Italians: they have to satisfy their love of colour and shape as well as of taste. The two recipes we have selected for you, Stuffed Peaches and Fresh Fruit Salad, will meet these standards, particularly if you improve their presentation still further by serving them in a pretty dish.

MENU

Italian Sour Dip with vegetable crudites

Veal Valdostana

Pasta Primavera

Italian Fresh Fruit Salad

coffee

white wine

Minestra di Pasta e Ceci

EXCHANGES PER SERVING:	1 Fat
	1½ Vegetable
	1½ Protein
	½ Bread

SERVES 2 (220 Calories per serving)

This pasta and chick pea soup is a typical thick Italian soup. For a change, use a different shaped pasta such as small shells (conchigliette) or tiny bows (fiochetti).

2 teaspoons olive oil

3oz (90g) onion, chopped

2 garlic cloves, finely chopped

6oz (180g) drained canned tomatoes, chopped

9oz (270g) drained canned chick peas, reserve 4fl oz (120ml) of the liquid

3oz (90g) cooked elbow macaroni

1½ teaspoons chopped basil

salt and pepper

basil sprig to garnish

Heat the oil in a saucepan over a medium heat. Add the onion and garlic and saute until the onion is translucent. Add the tomatoes and bring to the boil. Cover the saucepan, reduce the heat and simmer very gently for 5 minutes. Stir in the chick peas, the reserved liquid, macaroni, chopped basil and a good sprinkling of salt and pepper. Stir until heated through. Serve garnished with the sprig of basil.

Italian Sour Dip

SERVES 4 (115 Calories per serving)

Although expensive, it is worthwhile buying fresh Parmesan cheese and grating it yourself. It has a more pungent flavour than the drums of ready grated Parmesan.

8 drained, canned anchovy fillets, chopped

10fl oz (300ml) skimmed milk

2 tablespoons cornflour

1 tablespoon fresh oregano or ½ teaspoon dried

2oz (60g) Parmesan cheese, finely grated

salt and pepper

sprigs of oregano to garnish

Using a pestle and mortar, or in a small bowl and using the back of a spoon, mash the anchovy fillets to a puree.

Mix a little of the milk with the cornflour to form a smooth paste. Heat the remaining milk with the oregano over a low heat until steaming. Pour the hot milk into the cornflour paste, stirring all the time. Return the sauce to the saucepan and stir continually over a low heat until the sauce boils. Simmer 1–2 minutes until the sauce thickens. Add the anchovy puree and Parmesan cheese and stir until the cheese dissolves. Season to taste.

Pour the sauce into 4 individual dishes or 1 large bowl, approximately 10fl oz (300ml) capacity. Garnish with the fresh oregano and surround with vegetable crudites. Serve hot.

EXCHANGES PER SERVING:	¼ Milk
	½ Protein
	1½ Vegetable
	25 Calories Optional

Veal Valdostana

SERVES 4 (395 Calories per serving)

Breaded veal with cheese: a simple meal, quick to make and served with lemon wedges.

4 tablespoons dried breadcrumbs

3 tablespoons plain flour

½ teaspoon salt

pepper

4 × 4-oz (120-g) veal cutlets

1 egg, beaten with 2 tablespoons water

2 tablespoons vegetable oil

4oz (120g) Fontina or Gruyere cheese, grated

8 lemon wedges to garnish

Spread the breadcrumbs out on a plate, set aside. Season the flour with the salt and a sprinkling of pepper and turn each cutlet in the seasoned flour to coat all sides. Dip each cutlet in the egg and water mixture then turn in the breadcrumbs.

Heat 1 tablespoon oil in a medium-sized frying pan. Saute two of the veal cutlets in the hot fat until golden brown on each side. Preheat the grill on its highest setting. Keep the two browned cutlets warm while heating the remaining oil in the same frying pan and repeating the procedure with the other cutlets. Transfer all the veal to a baking sheet and sprinkle each cutlet with 1oz (30g) grated cheese. Place the baking sheet under the hot grill and cook the cutlets until the cheese has melted and is bubbling. Serve each portion on a warm plate garnished with 2 lemon wedges.

EXCHANGES PER SERVING: 4 Protein
1½ Fat
65 Calories Optional

Pasta Primavera

SERVES 4 (260 Calories per serving)

The assortment of vegetables mixed with cheese and pasta makes this a colourful and delightfully attractive dish.

10oz (300g) quark cheese

4fl oz (120ml) skimmed milk

4 teaspoons low-fat spread

3–4 garlic cloves, finely chopped

12oz (360g) cooked fettuccine, linguine or tagliatelli, hot

1 red pepper, seeded and cut into matchstick-sized pieces

4oz (120g) cooked, diagonally sliced asparagus

4oz (120g) cooked sliced carrots

4oz (120g) cooked sliced courgettes

2oz (60g) Parmesan cheese, grated

salt and pepper

Place the quark and milk in a blender or food processor and process until smooth, set aside.

Heat the low-fat spread over a medium heat until hot and bubbling. Add the garlic and saute briefly, do not brown. Pour the quark mixture into the pan and bring to the boil. Reduce the heat and stir in the remaining ingredients, seasoning well with salt and pepper. Toss well to coat the vegetables and pasta with the sauce. Serve as soon as the vegetables have heated through.

EXCHANGES PER SERVING: 1½ Protein
½ Fat
1 Bread
1½ Vegetable
25 Calories Optional

Left: Italian Fresh Fruit Salad (p 153)
Right: Mocha Cappuccino (p 154)
Bottom: Pasta Primavera

CHIANTI

Pasta e Piselli

SERVES 2 (280 Calories per serving)

Although called 'pasta and peas' this easy-to-prepare side dish is embellished with mushrooms, onion and cheese.

2 teaspoons olive oil or margarine

1½oz (45g) onion, chopped

1 garlic clove, finely chopped

1½oz (45g) mushrooms, sliced

8fl oz (240ml) tomato juice

3oz (90g) frozen petit pois

2oz (60g) Fontina or mozzarella cheese, grated

6oz (180g) cooked shell macaroni

5 teaspoons chopped parsley

salt and pepper

Heat the oil in a saucepan. Add the onion and garlic and saute 2–3 minutes until the onion is translucent. Add the mushrooms and saute over a very high heat until the liquid has evaporated. Stir in the tomato juice and bring to the boil. Simmer for about 15 minutes until the sauce has thickened slightly. Add the peas and cook for a further 3 minutes, stirring occasionally. Add all the remaining ingredients and season to taste with salt and pepper. Keep stirring until the cheese is melted. Serve immediately.

EXCHANGES PER SERVING: 1 Fat
1 Vegetable
½ Fruit
1 Protein
1 Bread

Bologneses Meat Sauce

SERVES 4 (145 Calories per serving)

This meat sauce tastes superb with any cooked pasta. It can be made in advance and stored in the refrigerator for up to three days, or it may be frozen for future use.

4 teaspoons olive oil
2 garlic cloves, finely chopped
3oz (90g) onion, chopped
1 medium carrot, finely chopped
1 stick celery, finely chopped
8oz (240g) minced veal
4fl oz (120ml) skimmed milk
1lb (480g) drained canned tomatoes, chopped
1 teaspoon salt
pepper
ground nutmeg

Heat the oil in a saucepan, add the garlic and onion and saute gently until the onion is translucent. Stir in the carrot and celery and cook for a further 2 minutes. Stir in the veal and, stirring constantly, continue cooking until the veal loses its pink colour. Add the milk and cook over a low heat until some of the liquid has evaporated, about 3 minutes. Stir in the remaining ingredients and bring to the boil. Reduce the heat and simmer, stirring occasionally, until the sauce is thick and creamy, about 30 minutes.

EXCHANGES PER SERVING: 1 Fat
2 Vegetable
1½ Protein
10 Calories Optional

Linguine Verdi ai Quattro Formaggi

SERVES 4 (325 Calories per serving)

Green linguine or tagliatelli served in a sauce made from four cheeses.

4oz (120g) quark cheese

2oz (60g) mozzarella cheese, grated

2oz (60g) Fontina or Gruyere cheese, grated

2oz (60g) Parmesan cheese, grated

3 tablespoons skimmed milk

2 tablespoons plus 2 teaspoons low-fat spread

12oz (360g) cooked hot spinach linguine or tagliatelli

salt and pepper

In a small saucepan heat the quark until thinned, stirring all the time with a wooden spoon. Gradually add the remaining cheeses, stirring well after each addition. When the cheeses have melted, add the milk, 1 tablespoon at a time, stirring thoroughly until blended. Keep warm over the lowest possible heat. In a separate saucepan melt the low-fat spread, pour over the hot linguine or tagliatelli and toss to combine. Transfer the pasta to a warm serving dish and pour over the hot cheese sauce, toss once again and season with a little salt and pepper.

EXCHANGES PER SERVING: 2 Protein
1 Fat
1 Bread
10 Calories Optional

Top: Minestra di Pasta e Ceci (p 143)
Bottom: Italian Sour Dip (p 144)

CHIANTI
BESSI
VIN ROUGE

Pesche Ripiene

SERVES 4 (225 Calories per serving)

Serve these delicious stuffed peaches warm or chilled.

4 medium peaches

2 tablespoons margarine

1 tablespoon caster sugar

1 tablespoon desiccated coconut

2 teaspoons cocoa

1 egg, beaten

½ teaspoon almond flavouring

4 digestive biscuits, crushed

3 tablespoons Marsala wine

Preheat the oven to 375°F, 190°C, Gas Mark 5. Cut the peaches in half and remove the stones. Scoop out some of the flesh from each peach with a teaspoon, leaving a sufficient border to retain the shape of the fruit. Chop the peach flesh and put to one side. In a small bowl mix together 4 teaspoons margarine with the sugar. When well blended stir in the coconut and cocoa. Stir in the egg, almond flavouring, digestive crumbs and reserved peach flesh, mix well.

Arrange the peaches, cut side up, in an ovenproof dish just large enough to hold the halves. Divide the stuffing evenly between the peach halves. Pour the wine into the dish and dot the remaining margarine round the peaches and in the wine. Bake in the preheated oven for 20–25 minutes until the peaches are beginning to brown. Serve warm or chilled with the juices from the dish poured over the peach halves.

EXCHANGES PER SERVING: 1 Fruit
1½ Fat
1 Bread
50 Calories Optional

Italian Fresh Fruit Salad

EXCHANGES PER SERVING: 1 Fruit
35 Calories Optional

SERVES 4 (70 Calories per serving)

A deliciously refreshing salad incorporating many Italian fruits.

zest of ½ a lemon, removed with a potato peeler

4fl oz (120ml) water

4 teaspoons sugar

1 tablespoon lemon juice

2 large figs, peeled and sliced

1 orange, segmented and membranes removed, reserving any juices which run

3oz (90g) grapes, halved and seeded

1 medium peach or nectarine, halved, stoned and sliced

5oz (150g) melon, cubed

Place the lemon zest, water and sugar in a small saucepan. Bring to the boil over a low heat and simmer for 1–2 minutes. Leave until cold, then add the lemon juice. Place all the prepared fruits in the serving bowl, remove the strips of lemon zest from the syrup and discard. Pour the syrup over the fruits and leave for the flavours to blend for 1–2 hours or longer.

Mocha Cappuccino

SERVES 4 (55 Calories per serving)

A very special coffee for a grand occasion.

2 cups strong coffee, hot

4 teaspoons cocoa

10fl oz (300ml) skimmed milk

4 tablespoons whipped dessert topping

ground cinnamon

Stir the coffee and cocoa together until the cocoa dissolves, pour into four cups. Heat the milk until steaming and pour into the coffee, stir. Top each cup with 1 tablespoon whipped dessert topping and sprinkle with a little ground cinnamon.

EXCHANGES PER SERVING: ¼ Milk
45 Calories Optional

NORTH AMERICA

The menus of North America with their diverse ethnic recipes reflect the history of the many immigrants who went to the shores of Canada and the United States. In their national melting pot, there is no real United States cuisine, but rather a myriad of regional specialities.

From New England comes one of the most famous dishes, Boston Baked Beans, traditionally made with white beans and dark molasses. From New Orleans comes Creole cookery – a lively and unique combination of provincial French and Spanish styles with an African accent. One of the best-known Creole dishes is Jambalaya, a rice dish customarily made with pork or ham and prawns, although other shellfish, and chicken, can be used. A coast to coast tradition is the pairing of fried potatoes with steak, a duo which dates back to colonial times, for it was Thomas Jefferson who concocted the idea. Our baked version of these 'fries' helps you declare your independence from the tyranny of excess pounds!

Much of Canada's cuisine mirrors her British ancestry, but French-speaking Quebec retains Gallic specialities like Tourtiere, a pie made with pork, veal or chicken. Because it's especially popular at Christmas, Tourtiere is also known as pâté de Nöel.

During the snowy Canadian winters, hot and nourishing soups are welcome, among them the chowder brought by the French settlers. The name comes from the chaudiere, or cauldron, in which it was cooked. Corn Chowder, relished throughout Canada, is also very popular in the southern United States, proving that culinary customs can migrate freely across borders!

MENU

Canadian Yellow Split Pea Soup

Jambalaya and mixed salad

Blueberry Crumble

coffee

white wine

Canadian Corn Chowder

SERVES 2 (280 Calories per serving)

A thick, warming soup for chilly winter nights.

2 teaspoons margarine

2oz (60g) boiled ham, diced

3oz (90g) onion, diced

2 tablespoons diced celery

2 tablespoons grated carrot

1½ teaspoons plain flour

4fl oz (120ml) skimmed milk

3oz (90g) potato, diced

½ teaspoon salt

marjoram leaves

pepper

9oz (270g) frozen or drained canned sweetcorn

water, if necessary

Heat the margarine in a saucepan until hot and bubbling. Add the ham, onion, celery and carrot and saute until the onion is translucent. Sprinkle in the flour and stir over a moderate heat for 1 minute. Gradually blend in the milk and bring to the boil, stirring all the time. Reduce the heat, add the potato and seasonings, cover and simmer gently for about 15 minutes until the potato is cooked. Stir in the sweetcorn and simmer until heated through. If the mixture gets too thick, add a little water, about a tablespoon at a time, until the desired consistency is obtained.

EXCHANGES PER SERVING: 1 Fat
1 Protein
1 Vegetable
2 Bread
30 Calories Optional

Jambalaya

SERVES 4 (335 Calories per serving)

The popularity of this dish spans time and distance, from seventeenth-century Acadia to current Creole cuisine.

2 teaspoons olive or vegetable oil

6oz (180g) onion, chopped

1 green pepper, seeded and chopped

3 garlic cloves, finely chopped

1lb (480g) large peeled prawns

4oz (120g) boiled ham, diced

2 × 14-oz (420-g) cans tomatoes, with liquid reserved and the tomatoes chopped

8fl oz (240ml) chicken stock

1 tablespoon lemon juice

1 bay leaf

paprika

thyme leaves

pepper

hot pepper sauce

4oz (120g) uncooked long grain rice

1 tablespoon chopped parsley to garnish

Heat the oil in a small frying pan, add the onion, pepper and garlic and cook until the onion is translucent. Remove from the heat and stir in the prawns and ham, set aside.

Place the tomatoes and their liquid in a saucepan. Stir in the stock, lemon juice, bay leaf and a sprinkling of paprika, thyme and pepper. Mix in the prawn and ham mixture and season with a dash of hot pepper sauce. Bring the mixture to the boil, stir in the rice and reduce the heat. Cover and simmer gently for about 20 minutes until the rice is cooked. Remove the bay leaf and serve sprinkled with chopped parsley.

EXCHANGES PER SERVING: ½ Fat
2 Vegetable
5 Protein
1 Bread

Top: Jambalaya
Bottom: Blueberry Crumble (p 170)

SERVE COLD
GENUINE

Boston Brown Bread

SERVES 8 (160 Calories per serving)

This bread is traditionally served with Boston Baked Beans (see page 161) but tastes equally good spread with margarine for breakfast.

4oz (120g) large seedless raisins, roughly chopped

5½oz (165g) wholewheat flour

2½oz (75g) cornmeal

1 teaspoon salt

4 tablespoons molasses

2 teaspoons water

½ teaspoon bicarbonate of soda

8fl oz (240ml) skimmed milk

1 tablespoon lemon juice

Line a 1lb (480g) coffee tin with non-stick baking parchment.

Sprinkle the raisins with 2 tablespoons flour. Mix the remaining flour with the cornmeal and salt in a large mixing bowl. Stir the molasses, water and bicarbonate of soda together in a small bowl until smooth, foamy and caramel-coloured. Pour the molasses into the flour and mix well. Stir the milk and lemon juice together and mix into the flour and molasses. Stir the raisins into the batter, then pour into the prepared tin. Cover tightly with foil, then transfer to a large saucepan. Stand the tin on a rack or upturned plate and pour sufficient boiling water into the saucepan to reach halfway up the tin. Cover and simmer for 2½–3 hours. Test to check the bread is cooked by inserting a metal skewer into it. If it comes out clean, remove the bread from the saucepan, if not return for a further 10–15 minutes then repeat the test. Turn the bread out and allow to cool slightly before cutting into eight equal slices.

EXCHANGES PER SERVING: ½ Fruit
1 Bread
40 Calories Optional

Boston Baked Beans

EXCHANGES PER SERVING: 1 Protein
½ Vegetable
40 Calories Optional

SERVES 2 (115 Calories per serving)

Serve this dish with a slice of Boston Brown Bread (page 160).

6oz (180g) drained, canned haricot beans

4fl oz (120ml) water or stock

2 tablespoons finely chopped onion

2½ teaspoons molasses

½ teaspoon powdered mustard

large pinch ground ginger

pinch ground cloves

1½ teaspoons dark brown sugar

Preheat the oven to 350°F, 180°C, Gas Mark 4. Mix together all the ingredients except the brown sugar and place in a small flameproof casserole. Cover and bake in the preheated oven for 40–45 minutes until hot and bubbling. Preheat the grill on a medium setting. Remove the casserole from the oven, sprinkle the sugar evenly over the beans and place under the preheated grill until the sugar is bubbling.

Canadian Yellow Split Pea Soup

SERVES 4 (195 Calories per serving)

Sage and allspice lend an accent to this bacon-flavoured soup.

4oz (120g) uncooked yellow split peas

2 teaspoons vegetable oil

6oz (180g) onions, chopped

4oz (120g) carrots, sliced

6oz (180g) potatoes, diced small

2oz (60g) boiled ham, diced

1½ pints (900ml) chicken stock

¼ teaspoon sage

¼ teaspoon ground allspice

salt and pepper

2 tablespoons chopped parsley to garnish

Rinse the peas, cover with boiling water and leave to soak for 1 hour, drain.

Heat the oil in a saucepan. Add the onions and carrots and cook, stirring occasionally, until the onions are translucent. Remove from the heat and stir in the drained peas, potatoes, ham, chicken stock, sage and allspice. Season with a little salt and pepper and return to a medium heat. Bring to the boil, reduce the heat to low and simmer gently, stirring from time to time until the peas soften and the soup thickens, about 45 minutes. Pour into a warm soup tureen and sprinkle with parsley before serving.

EXCHANGES PER SERVING: 1 Protein
½ Fat
1 Vegetable
½ Bread
25 Calories Optional

Vegetable Medley Canadian Style

EXCHANGES PER SERVING: 1½ Fat
1½ Vegetable
5 Calories Optional

SERVES 2 (85 Calories per serving)

A touch of lemon, sugar and dillweed make this an extra special vegetable accompaniment.

1 tablespoon margarine

4oz (120g) carrots, sliced

3oz (90g) onions, diced

2oz (60g) celery, diced

¼ teaspoon granulated sugar

¼ teaspoon dillweed

a little grated lemon zest

Melt the margarine in a saucepan. Add all the remaining ingredients and stir to coat the vegetables with the margarine. Reduce the heat to the lowest possible setting, cover the saucepan and cook until the vegetables are tender, 10–15 minutes. Serve the vegetables with any remaining pan juices.

Orange-Date Bread

SERVES 8 (220 Calories per serving)

This versatile bread is suitable as a dessert or snack, or it can be toasted and spread with low-calorie marmalade or cottage cheese to make an interesting breakfast.

8oz (240g) plain flour

2 teaspoons baking powder

½ teaspoon salt

3 tablespoons caster sugar

1 tablespoon grated orange zest

8fl oz (240ml) orange juice

4 tablespoons margarine, melted

1 egg, beaten

8 dates, stoned and chopped

Preheat the oven to 350°F, 180°C, Gas Mark 4. Line a 1lb (480g) loaf tin with baking parchment. Sieve the flour, baking powder and salt into a mixing bowl. Stir in the sugar and orange zest. In a small bowl, beat together the orange juice, margarine and egg, pour into the dry ingredients and stir well to combine. Fold in the dates. Transfer the mixture to the prepared loaf tin and bake in the preheated oven for 50–60 minutes. Test to ensure the bread is cooked by inserting a metal skewer into the centre of the bread. If it comes out clean it is cooked, if not return to the oven and test once again after a few minutes. Remove the bread from the loaf tin, transfer to a wire rack and leave for at least 10 minutes before slicing. To serve, cut into eight equal slices.

EXCHANGES PER SERVING: 1 Bread
½ Fruit
1½ Fat
45 Calories Optional

Tourtiere

SERVES 8 (360 Calories per serving)

This pork pie is a particular favourite in Canada.

FOR THE PASTRY:

8oz (240g) plain flour
½ teaspoon salt
4 tablespoons plus 2 teaspoons margarine
4fl oz (120ml) low-fat natural yogurt
1 tablespoon flour for rolling out pastry

FOR THE FILLING:

2 teaspoons vegetable oil
3oz (90g) onion, diced
2 garlic cloves, finely chopped
1¼lbs (600g) minced pork, made into patties, grilled and crumbled
12oz (360g) cooked potatoes, mashed
1 teaspoon salt
½ teaspoon sage
½ teaspoon ground nutmeg
¼ teaspoon pepper

FOR THE GLAZE:

½ egg, beaten

To prepare the pastry: Sieve together the flour and salt. Rub in the margarine until the mixture resembles coarse breadcrumbs. Mix in the yogurt to form the pastry dough. Divide the pastry into two equal balls and wrap in clingfilm, refrigerate for at least an hour.

To prepare the filling: Heat the oil in a small frying pan over a medium heat. Add the onion and garlic and saute until the onion is golden. Transfer the onion and garlic to a mixing bowl and add the remaining filling ingredients, stir well to combine.

To assemble the pie: Preheat the oven to 425°F, 210°C, Gas Mark 7. Use the extra tablespoon of flour to flour the board and sprinkle on the pastry. Roll each ball of pastry to form circles large enough to line an 8–9-inch (20–23-cm) pie plate or flan dish. Use one circle to line the pie plate. Spoon the filling into the lined tin. Dampen the edge of the pastry. Place the second pastry circle over the filling and press the edges together. Flute or flake the edges to help them to seal. Brush the pastry with the beaten egg and make a small hole in the centre to allow the steam to escape. Bake in the preheated oven for 25–30 minutes until golden brown.

EXCHANGES PER SERVING: 1½ Bread
2 Fat
½ Vegetable
2 Protein
15 Calories Optional

Orange and Sultana Cheesecake (p 169)

Oven-Baked Steak 'Fries'

SERVES 2 (95 Calories per serving)

Our own version of the ever-popular 'French fries'.

6oz (180g) potato, cut into ½-inch (1-cm) wedges

1 teaspoon vegetable oil

1 teaspoon paprika

salt and pepper

Preheat the oven to 425°F, 210°C, Gas Mark 7. Using a pastry brush, brush all the sides of the potato wedges with oil. Arrange the potato on a non-stick baking sheet and sprinkle with the paprika, salt and pepper to taste. Bake in the preheated oven until the wedges are brown and tender, 15–20 minutes.

EXCHANGES PER SERVING: 1 Bread
½ Fat

Orange and Sultana Cheesecake

SERVES 8 (215 Calories per serving)

This cheesecake is very easy to make and if you don't have a 7-inch (18-cm) flan dish, line a sandwich tin with foil or baking parchment.

8 small digestive biscuits, crushed
8 teaspoons margarine, melted
12oz (360g) cottage cheese, sieved or low-fat soft cheese
2 eggs
1 tablespoon caster sugar
2 tablespoons self-raising flour
4fl oz (120ml) orange juice
1 teaspoon grated orange zest
3oz (90g) sultanas

Mix together the crushed biscuits and melted margarine, spoon into a 7-inch (18-cm) flan dish or lined sandwich tin. Press firmly with the back of a spoon. Refrigerate for about an hour. Preheat the oven to 325°F, 160°C, Gas Mark 3. Beat together the cheese, eggs, caster sugar and flour. Gradually beat in the orange juice and zest to form a smooth mixture. Stir in the sultanas and spoon the mixture over the crumb base. Bake in the preheated oven for 1 hour, remove from the oven and allow to cool completely before cutting. If the cheesecake has been made in a lined tin, remove the cold cheesecake from the tin, peel away the foil or baking parchment, then cut into eight slices.

EXCHANGES PER SERVING: 1 Bread
1 Fat
1 Protein
½ Fruit
15 Calories Optional

Blueberry Crumble

SERVES 4 (250 Calories per serving)

Serve this delicious Canadian dessert warm, on its own or with a little low-fat natural yogurt.

1lb 4oz (600g) blueberries, fresh or frozen

1 tablespoon lemon juice

2 tablespoons dark brown sugar

1 tablespoon cornflour

4oz (120g) porridge oats

3 tablespoons plain flour

ground cinnamon

8 teaspoons margarine, softened

Preheat the oven to 350°F, 180°C, Gas Mark 4. Mix together the blueberries and lemon juice. In a separate bowl, stir 1 tablespoon sugar and the cornflour together, mix into the blueberries and transfer to a shallow casserole or ovenproof dish. Mix together the porridge oats, flour, the remaining sugar and a sprinkling of cinnamon. With a pastry blender or fork, work the margarine into the oat mixture until evenly distributed. Sprinkle over the blueberries and bake in the preheated oven for 25–30 minutes until the berries are bubbling and the crumbs lightly browned.

EXCHANGES PER SERVING: 1 Fruit
1 Bread
2 Fat
60 Calories Optional

RUSSIA

Because this enormous land blends both European and Asian tastes, there isn't just one Russian cuisine, there are many. From the agriculturally rich Ukraine, once known as the 'bread basket of the world', comes grain for the hearty dark Russian breads and the traditional Kasha, which can be served at breakfast or as a main dish accompaniment, a side dish or stuffing. Yogurt and kefir (fermented milk), Russian staples today, originated with the nomadic tribes of the eastern steppes.

In the legendary sub-zero winters, meals need to be hot and nourishing, although Borsch, the national soup (based on cabbage and beetroot), may be served either hot or cold. Some dishes bear the names of noblemen, but Kotlety Pozharskie, popular minced chicken patties, were named after the innkeeper who invented them.

Caviar remains an expensive delicacy, traditionally obtained by cutting holes in the ice to harpoon sturgeons for their roe, but you won't have to worry about the method or the cost of our delicious alternative: Aubergine 'Caviar'. This makes a very tasty starter.

Blini are little pancakes usually eaten with sour cream. We serve ours with strawberry jam, but they can equally be enjoyed with other fillings, sweet and savoury.

The Russians share with most of the world a love of desserts. Sample their Kisel, an apple pudding, and don't forget to wash it all down with hot black tea, drunk from glasses in true Russian style.

MENU

Borsch Ukrainsky

Codfish Cakes with Mustard Sauce

carrots

Kasha

Kisel

lemon tea

vodka

Aubergine 'Caviar'

SERVES 4 (90 Calories per serving)

Serve with thin slices of bread, melba toast or crispbread.

1½lbs aubergines

4 teaspoons olive oil

6oz (180g) onions, chopped

½ green pepper, chopped

2 garlic cloves, finely chopped

2 tomatoes, peeled, seeded and finely chopped

½ teaspoon salt

½ teaspoon sugar

¼ teaspoon pepper

4½ teaspoons lemon juice

Preheat the oven to 400°F, 200°C, Gas Mark 6. Lay the aubergines on a rack placed in the roasting pan and bake in the preheated oven, turning once or twice, until soft and well charred, about 30 minutes. Allow to cool until easy to handle, then peel away the skin and chop the pulp.

Heat 2 teaspoons oil in a large frying pan which has a lid to cover it. Add the onions and saute until translucent. Stir in the pepper and garlic and cook for a further 5 minutes, transfer the sauted vegetables to a mixing bowl and stir in the aubergine pulp, chopped tomatoes, salt, sugar and pepper.

Heat the remaining oil in the same frying pan, add the aubergine mixture and bring to the boil, stirring all the time. Reduce the heat, cover the pan and cook for half an hour, stirring occasionally. Remove the cover and simmer for a further 5 minutes, stirring occasionally until the mixture is thick. Stir in the lemon juice. Spoon the mixture into a serving bowl and leave to cool. Cover and refrigerate for at least 4 hours.

EXCHANGES PER SERVING: 3 Vegetable
1 Fat
5 Calories Optional

Borsch Ukrainsky

SERVES 6 as a snack meal (230 Calories per serving)
SERVES 12 as a starter (115 Calories per serving)

This Ukrainian-style soup can be a filling snack meal or served as a starter at a Russian dinner party.

1lb (480g) lean chuck steak

1 tablespoon vegetable oil

2½ pints (1 litre 500ml) beef stock

12oz (360g) cabbage, finely grated

9oz (270g) uncooked beetroot, finely grated

2 tomatoes, peeled and chopped

4oz (120g) carrots, sliced

3oz (90g) onions, chopped

1½ teaspoons cider vinegar

2 tablespoons tomato puree

1 tablespoon chopped parsley

1 tablespoon chopped dill

9oz (270g) potatoes, diced

½ teaspoon salt

pepper

6 fl oz (180ml) or 12 tablespoons low-fat natural yogurt, stirred

Place the meat on the rack of a grill pan and grill, turning once, until rare. Cut into 1-inch (2.5-cm) cubes.

Heat the oil in a large saucepan, add the meat in batches and sear on all sides. Pour in the stock, vegetables, vinegar, tomato puree and herbs. Cover the pan and simmer for about 1 hour. Stir in the potatoes, salt and a sprinkling of pepper, cover and simmer for a further 20–30 minutes. Ladle the borsch into warm bowls and top each portion with 2 tablespoons yogurt if serving as a snack meal, or 1 tablespoon yogurt if serving as a starter.

EXCHANGES PER SERVING: (for 6)	2 Protein ½ Fat 2 Vegetable ½ Bread 25 Calories Optional

Top: Borsch Ukrainsky
Bottom: Blini (p 176)

Blini

EXCHANGES PER SERVING: 1 Bread
½ Protein
1 Fat
60 Calories Optional

SERVES 2 (235 Calories per serving)

Traditionally these little pancakes are made with buckwheat and plain flour, but this recipe can be made with ingredients from most people's store cupboard.

2oz (60g) plain flour

½ teaspoon baking powder

pinch of salt

1½ teaspoons caster sugar

1 large egg

2½fl oz (75ml) or 5 tablespoons low-fat natural yogurt

1 teaspoon margarine, melted

1 teaspoon vegetable oil

4 teaspoons low-calorie strawberry jam

Sieve the flour, baking powder and salt into a bowl. Stir in the sugar. In a small bowl, beat together the egg, 3 tablespoons yogurt and the margarine. Gradually blend into the dry ingredients to make a smooth thick batter. Heat the oil in a large non-stick frying pan and drop tablespoons of the batter to form six pancakes about 3 inches (7.5cm) in diameter. Cook until the bottom is golden brown, turn over and cook the other side. Serve each portion with 1 tablespoon yogurt and 2 teaspoons strawberry jam.

Kasha

SERVES 6 (145 Calories per serving)

This is the staff of life in Russia.

6oz (180g) buckwheat groats (kasha)

1 large egg, lightly beaten

2 tablespoons low-fat spread

6oz (180g) onions, chopped

6oz (180g) mushrooms, sliced

16fl oz (480ml) water or vegetable or chicken stock, boiling

¼ teaspoon salt

Mix the buckwheat and egg together in a bowl. Heat the low-fat spread in a saucepan until hot and bubbling. Add the onions and saute until softened. Add the mushrooms and saute for a further 2 minutes. Stir in the buckwheat and stir constantly over a medium heat for 3 minutes, taking care not to burn the grains. Pour in the boiling water or stock, add the salt, cover and simmer for 15 minutes until the liquid has been absorbed and the buckwheat is cooked.

EXCHANGES PER SERVING: 1 Bread
½ Fat
1 Vegetable
25 Calories Optional

Codfish Cakes with Mustard Sauce

SERVES 6 (250 Calories per serving)

The dill-flavoured tangy mustard sauce is the perfect complement to codfish.

1lb 14oz (900g) cod fillets, skinned and cut into 2-inch (5-cm) pieces

4oz (120g) onion, finely chopped

3 × 1-oz (30-g) slices white bread, made into crumbs and soaked in 3 tablespoons skimmed milk

8 tablespoons chopped dill

salt and pepper

3 tablespoons plain flour

3 tablespoons Dijon-style mustard

3 tablespoons water

1 tablespoon cucumber relish

1 tablespoon lemon juice

3 tablespoons vegetable oil

5 tablespoons chopped parsley

Process the cod and onion in a food processor until smooth. Add the soaked crumbs, half the dill and a sprinkling of salt and pepper, process until smooth. Form the mixture into 12 equal patties and sprinkle both sides of each patty with ¼ teaspoon flour. Cover and refrigerate the patties for 30–40 minutes.

Mix together the mustard, water, relish, lemon juice, 1 teaspoon oil and the parsley. Season with a little salt and pepper and add the remaining dill, pour into a sauce boat or dish and set aside.

Heat the remaining oil in a large frying pan. Add the fish cakes and cook, turning once, until golden brown, about 3 minutes on each side. Serve the hot fishcakes with the mustard sauce.

EXCHANGES PER SERVING: 4 Protein
½ Vegetable
½ Bread
1½ Fat
30 Calories Optional

Kotlety Pozharskie

SERVES 4 (285 Calories per serving)

Turn your dinner into a Russian repast with these sauted chicken patties.

4 × 1-oz (30-g) slices white bread

4 tablespoons skimmed milk

1¼lbs (600g) skinned and boned chicken breasts, chopped

5 teaspoons margarine

½ teaspoon salt

large pinch pepper

Crumble 2 slices of bread into a small bowl, add the milk and leave to soak for 5 minutes.

Place the chicken, the soaked bread, 2 teaspoons margarine, salt and pepper in a food processor and process to a paste. Using damp hands, shape the chicken mixture into four equal-sized patties the shape of chops and about ¾ inch (2cm) thick.

Process the remaining bread to make breadcrumbs. Turn the chicken patties in the fresh breadcrumbs, pressing them on firmly to coat the mixture. Heat the remaining margarine in a large frying pan until hot and bubbling. Add the patties and saute, turning once, until the chicken is cooked and golden, about 5 minutes each side.

EXCHANGES PER SERVING: 1 Bread
4 Protein
1 Fat
20 Calories Optional

Sauted Liver, Potatoes and Mushrooms

SERVES 2 (325 Calories per serving)

A meal which can be quickly made in one pan and served with a crisp salad.

2 teaspoons margarine

2oz (60g) onions, sliced and separated into rings

6oz (180g) cooked potatoes, cut into ¼-inch (5-mm) thick slices

3–4oz (90–120g) mushrooms, halved

salt and pepper

2 teaspoons plain flour

10oz (300g) calf or lamb's liver, sliced

4fl oz (120ml) vegetable stock

¼ teaspoon tomato paste

1fl oz (30ml) or 2 tablespoons low-fat natural yogurt

Heat 1 teaspoon margarine in a medium-sized frying pan until hot and bubbling. Add the onion rings and saute until translucent. Add the potato and mushrooms and sprinkle with a little salt and pepper, saute until the vegetables are lightly browned. Remove from the pan and keep warm.

Season the flour with a sprinkling of salt and pepper. Turn the liver slices in the seasoned flour. Heat the remaining margarine in the same frying pan, add the liver and saute, turning once, until cooked according to taste. Stir in the stock and tomato paste and bring to the boil. Return the potato mixture to the pan and heat through. Stir in the yogurt and allow to heat through, but do not boil or the sauce will curdle.

EXCHANGES PER SERVING: 1 Fat
1 Vegetable
1 Bread
4 Protein
20 Calories Optional

Russian Krupnik

EXCHANGES PER SERVING: 2½ Protein
1 Vegetable
15 Calories Optional

SERVES 4 (220 Calories per serving)

An economical beef and barley stew suitable for a midday or evening meal.

8oz (240g) chuck steak, cut into cubes
2 pints (1 litre 200ml) beef stock
4oz (120g) carrots, cut into chunks
2oz (60g) celery, cut into chunks
1 onion, cut into chunks
2oz (60g) pearl barley, rinsed
2oz (60g) lentils, rinsed
1 bay leaf
salt and pepper
3oz (90g) drained canned chick peas

Place the meat on the rack of a grill pan and grill, turning to brown all sides, until rare. Place the meat and all the remaining ingredients except the chick peas in a large saucepan, cover and simmer for about 50 minutes until the meat is tender. Stir in the chick peas and simmer for a further 3–4 minutes until heated through. Remove the bay leaf before serving.

Chicken with Prune Sauce

SERVES 2 (275 Calories per serving)

The lemony prune sauce gives a piquancy to the chicken.

1 teaspoon vegetable oil

2 × 8-oz (240-g) chicken legs, skinned

salt and pepper

2oz (60g) onion, chopped

2oz (60g) celery, chopped

2oz (60g) carrot, chopped

5fl oz (150ml) water

parsley sprig

½ bay leaf

4 large stoned prunes, soaked

¾ teaspoon lemon juice

¼ teaspoon sugar

1 teaspoon margarine

1 teaspoon plain flour

Heat the oil in a large frying pan or large shallow saucepan. Add the chicken, sprinkle with a little salt and pepper and saute until lightly browned on all sides. Remove the chicken and set aside. Stir the vegetables into the pan and saute until soft but not browned. Return the chicken to the pan with 4 tablespoons water, the parsley and bay leaf and bring to the boil. Reduce the heat, cover and simmer gently until the chicken is tender, about 20 minutes. During the last 10 minutes that the chicken is cooking, combine the remaining water, prunes, lemon juice and sugar in a small saucepan. Simmer over a low heat until the prunes are tender, about 5 minutes.

Transfer the chicken to a warmed serving dish, reserve the vegetable mixture and discard the parsley and bay leaf. Arrange the prunes around the chicken, reserve the prune cooking liquid. Cover the dish with foil and keep warm. Sieve the vegetable mixture into a bowl, press the vegetables to extract as much liquid as possible, reserve the liquid and discard the solids. Heat the margarine until hot and bubbling in a small saucepan, add the flour and stir constantly over a low heat for 2 minutes. Gradually stir in the reserved vegetable and prune liquid and, stirring constantly, bring to the boil and cook until thickened. Adjust the seasoning and pour the smooth thick sauce over the chicken and prunes before serving.

EXCHANGES PER SERVING: 1 Fat
5 Protein
1 Vegetable
1 Fruit
10 Calories Optional

Kisel

SERVES 4 (80 Calories per serving)

A thick and creamy apple pudding.

1½ teaspoons potato flour or cornflour

12fl oz (360ml) water

4 medium cooking apples, cored, peeled and cut into ½-inch (1-cm) slices

2 tablespoons sugar

Mix the potato flour with 3 tablespoons water, set aside. Place the apple slices in a small saucepan with the remaining water and bring to the boil. Reduce the heat and simmer until the apples are tender, about 10 minutes. Sieve or liquidise the stewed apples then return the puree to the saucepan and stir in the sugar. Bring to the boil and stir in the potato flour, boil 2–3 minutes, stirring all the time. Allow to cool until just lukewarm, then pour into 4 dessert dishes, chill, cover and refrigerate for at least 4 hours.

EXCHANGES PER SERVING: 1 Fruit
35 Calories Optional

SCANDINAVIA

The smorgasbord is undoubtedly the single best-known Scandinavian speciality. Swedish etiquette requires at least three trips to the table: first for fish, then for cold meats and salads, and third (but not necessarily last!) for hot dishes. However, the weight-conscious Swedes are modifying their approach and in restaurants today there is a simplified 'one trip' version in which half a dozen items are placed on a single plate.

Although the Scandinavian countries have individual specialities, they share a talent for design, not just in tableware but also in the presentation of food. They also share a love of fish: the Vastkustsallad, a mixture of prawns and mussels with mushrooms and lettuce, will give you a taste of typical west coast fare.

Beef is also enjoyed in Scandinavia, particularly in dishes like the Swedish Meatballs and Beef a la Lindstrom. Nourishing hot soups are popular on the long winter nights, and chilled fruit soups are eaten on the warmer days of summer. Our two choices are Cauliflower Soup and Orange Soup.

Desserts are usually fresh fruit, and among them cloudberries are much liked. However, since this fruit is not easily available in this country we have selected Omenapuuro, a rice and apple porridge which is quite delicious served warm, and a fresh tasting Fluffy Orange Sundae.

MENU

Cauliflower Soup

Swedish Meatballs

noodles, broccoli and carrots

Fluffy Orange Sundae

coffee

Orange Soup

SERVES 4 (80 Calories per serving)

This delicious soup may be served warm or chilled. For the true Finnish flavour, use freshly squeezed orange juice.

1 tablespoon cornflour

1 teaspoon granulated sugar

8fl oz (240ml) water

16fl oz (480ml) orange juice

4 tablespoons whipped dessert topping

orange zest, cut into very thin strips, grated or removed with a zester to garnish

Gradually blend the cornflour, sugar and water together. Bring to the boil over a medium heat, stirring constantly until the mixture thickens. Remove from the heat and stir in the orange juice. Serve immediately or cover, refrigerate and serve chilled.

To serve, ladle the soup into four soup bowls and top each serving with a tablespoon of the whipped topping. Garnish with the strips of orange peel.

EXCHANGES PER SERVING: 1 Fruit
45 Calories Optional

Cauliflower Soup

SERVES 4 (115 Calories per serving)

Norwegians warm up with this soup on chilly winter evenings.

1lb 4oz (600g) cauliflower florets

16fl oz (480ml) chicken stock

2 tablespoons margarine

3oz (90g) onion, chopped

2 teaspoons plain flour

8fl oz (240ml) skimmed milk

salt and pepper

ground nutmeg (optional)

Boil the cauliflower in the stock until tender. Allow to cool slightly, then process in batches in a blender or food processor.

Heat the margarine in a saucepan until hot and bubbling. Stir in the onion and saute until translucent. Stir in the flour and cook for 1 minute over a moderate heat, stirring all the time. Gradually blend in the milk and bring to the boil, stirring constantly, until the liquid thickens. Stir in the pureed cauliflower, reduce the heat and simmer gently, stirring occasionally, until the cauliflower is heated through. Season to taste with salt and pepper. To serve, ladle into four warm soup bowls and sprinkle with ground nutmeg if desired.

EXCHANGES PER SERVING: 2 Vegetable
1½ Fat
25 Calories Optional

Danish Liver Pate

SERVES 4 (235 Calories per serving)

This homemade pate is simple to make and great for entertaining.

4 teaspoons margarine

3oz (90g) onion, finely chopped

5 teaspoons plain flour

8fl oz (240ml) skimmed milk

8oz (240g) lamb's or calf liver, finely minced

2 eggs, beaten

½ teaspoon salt

TO GARNISH:

½ medium tomato, thinly sliced

4 lettuce leaves, shredded

Preheat the oven to 375°F, 190°C, Gas Mark 5.

Heat the margarine in a medium-sized frying pan until hot and bubbling. Add the onion and saute until translucent. Sprinkle in the flour and cook for a minute, stirring all the time. Remove from the heat and gradually blend in the milk. Bring to the boil, stirring constantly, and simmer gently over a low heat until the mixture thickens. Allow to cool for a few minutes, then add the minced liver, eggs and salt and mix well. Transfer the mixture to a non-stick 1lb (480g) loaf tin and smooth over the surface. Bake in the centre of the preheated oven for 45–55 minutes until the mixture is set and the top is browned. Transfer the tin to a wire rack and leave to cool 5–10 minutes.

Invert the pate onto a serving plate and cover with clingfilm. Allow to cool, then refrigerate until thoroughly chilled, about 4 hours.

To serve, arrange the tomato slices along the centre of the pate and surround with the shredded lettuce.

EXCHANGES PER SERVING: 1 Fat
½ Vegetable
2 Protein
45 Calories Optional

Fruit Slaw

EXCHANGES PER SERVING: 1 Vegetable
¾ Fat
½ Fruit
10 Calories Optional

SERVES 4 (65 Calories per serving)

Orange segments, chopped apple and halved grapes make this a really special slaw.

4 tablespoons buttermilk

2 tablespoons low-calorie mayonnaise

2 teaspoons lemon juice

1 teaspoon cider vinegar

¼ teaspoon caraway seeds

salt and pepper

8oz (240g) white cabbage, finely shredded

1 medium apple, cored and diced

1½oz (45g) seedless grapes, halved

½ an orange, divided into segments and halved

1oz (30g) spring onions, sliced

Mix together the buttermilk, mayonnaise, lemon juice, vinegar and caraway seeds. Season to taste with salt and pepper. Add the remaining ingredients and toss well. Cover with clingfilm and refrigerate for at least 30 minutes. Toss again before serving.

Top: Fruit Slaw
Bottom: Fluffy Orange Sundae (p 198)

Beef a la Lindstrom

SERVES 4 (350 Calories per serving)

Serve these beef patties topped with 'fried' eggs for lunch or supper with a mixed salad.

1 teaspoon vegetable oil

3oz (90g) finely chopped onion

5 eggs

14oz (420g) minced beef

6oz (180g) cooked potatoes, mashed

3oz (90g) drained canned beetroot, chopped

3 tablespoons chopped capers

2 tablespoons finely chopped parsley

1 tablespoon red wine vinegar

1 tablespoon Worcestershire sauce

1 teaspoon salt

½ teaspoon pepper

Heat half the oil in a medium-sized frying pan. Add the onion and saute 2–3 minutes until soft. Beat one egg in a mixing bowl, stir in the cooked onion, minced beef, potatoes, beetroot, capers, parsley, vinegar, Worcestershire sauce and seasonings and mix well.

Preheat the grill on its highest setting. Shape the meat mixture into four even-sized patties and place on the grill pan rack. Grill the patties for 5–7 minutes, or until cooked, turning once.

While the patties are cooking, heat the remaining oil in the frying pan and cook the remaining four eggs. Serve each patty topped with a cooked egg.

EXCHANGES PER SERVING: ¼ Fat
½ Vegetable
4 Protein
½ Bread

Swedish Meatballs

SERVES 4 (420 Calories per serving)

These meatballs are simple to make and popular throughout the world.

4 teaspoons margarine

3oz (90g) onion, finely chopped

2oz (60g) skimmed milk powder, made up to 8fl oz (240ml) with cold water

1 egg, beaten

1oz (30g) fresh breadcrumbs

1lb (480g) minced beef

4oz (120g) minced pork

1½ teaspoons salt

½ teaspoon ground allspice

¼ teaspoon ground nutmeg

3 tablespoons plain flour

8fl oz (240ml) water

pepper

Preheat the oven to 350°F, 180°C, Gas Mark 4.

Heat 1 teaspoon margarine in a small frying pan, add the onion and saute until translucent. Mix together the onion, 4 tablespoons skimmed milk, egg and breadcrumbs. Leave to stand 5 minutes. Stir in the minced beef and pork, 1 teaspoon salt, the allspice and nutmeg and mix well.

Using a heaped tablespoon of the mixture, shape the meat into twenty meatballs. Place the meatballs on a rack standing in a roasting tin and bake in the preheated oven for 15–20 minutes, turning once.

While the meatballs are in the oven, melt the remaining margarine in a saucepan. Stir in the flour and gradually blend in the remaining skimmed milk, water, salt and a sprinkling of pepper. Bring to the boil, stirring all the time. Stir the baked meatballs into the sauce and simmer gently for about 3 minutes, stirring constantly.

EXCHANGES PER SERVING: 1 Fat
¼ Vegetable
½ Milk
4 Protein
¼ Bread
45 Calories Optional

Smorrebrod

SERVES 12 (305 Calories per serving)

In Denmark an open sandwich is called a smorrebrod. It's ideal for a party as the guests have the work of making their own sandwiches!

lettuce leaves

6 hard boiled eggs, cut in quarters

4oz (120g) peeled prawns

3oz (90g) smoked salmon, thinly sliced

3oz (90g) canned drained sardines, thinly sliced

2oz (60g) boiled ham, sliced

2oz (60g) rare roast beef, sliced

2oz (60g) Danish blue cheese, cubed

2oz (60g) Edam cheese, cubed

3 medium tomatoes, sliced

3 medium apples, cored, cut in wedges and turned in 2 teaspoons lemon juice

3 medium oranges, divided into segments with membranes removed

2oz (60g) onions, thinly sliced

24 pimento-stuffed green olives

6 gherkins, cut in quarters lengthways

4 tablespoons mayonnaise

4 tablespoons prepared mustard

4 tablespoons horseradish sauce

4 tablespoons seafood cocktail sauce

24 × ½-oz (15-g) slices rye bread

Line wooden serving boards or trays with the lettuce leaves. On each board or tray, decoratively arrange half the sandwich topping ingredients – the eggs, prawns, smoked salmon, sardines, ham, beef, cheeses, fruits and vegetables. Spoon the mayonnaise, mustard, horseradish sauce and seafood cocktail sauce into individual dishes. Cover the trays and bowls of sauces with clingfilm until just before serving.

To serve, set out the trays beside the sauce bowls and remove the clingfilm. Place the rye bread in one or two napkin-lined baskets.

EXCHANGES PER SERVING: 2 Protein
½ Vegetable
½ Fruit
1 Fat
1 Bread
45 Calories Optional

Vastkust-sallad

SERVES 4 (115 Calories per serving)

Prawns and mussels combine with dill to make this wonderful west coast salad a piquant treat from the waters of Scandinavia.

6oz (180g) peeled prawns

8oz (240g) mussels, steamed and shelled

3oz (90g) mushrooms, sliced

FOR THE DRESSING:

4 tablespoons water

4 teaspoons olive oil

1 tablespoon lemon juice

1 tablespoon red wine vinegar

2 teaspoons finely chopped dill

1 teaspoon Dijon-style mustard

2 garlic cloves, crushed

¼ teaspoon salt

¼ teaspoon pepper

4oz (120g) shredded lettuce to garnish

In a mixing bowl (not metal), mix together the prawns, mussels and mushrooms. Whisk all the dressing ingredients together in a separate small bowl or shake well in a screw top jar. Pour the dressing over the prawns and other ingredients and toss well. Cover the bowl with clingfilm and refrigerate for at least 2 hours. Stir once again before serving on a bed of shredded lettuce.

EXCHANGES PER SERVING: 2 Protein
1 Vegetable
1 Fat

Omena-puuro

SERVES 2 (190 Calories per serving)

This apple porridge dessert is a Finnish version of our rice pudding. It is served warm.

EXCHANGES PER SERVING:	1 Bread
	½ Fruit
	¼ Milk
	50 Calories Optional

2oz (60g) long grain rice

3fl oz (90ml) water

1 medium apple, peeled, cored and chopped

½oz (15g) skimmed milk powder made up to 3fl oz (90ml) with cold water

1½ teaspoons caster sugar

1½-inch (4-cm) cinnamon stick

1 strip of lemon peel, blanched

2 tablespoons whipped dessert topping

Place the rice and water in a small saucepan and bring to the boil. Reduce the heat to low, cover the pan and simmer gently for 10 minutes. Stir in all the remaining ingredients, except the dessert topping, cover and simmer for a further 15 minutes or until the rice is tender. Remove the cinnamon stick and lemon peel and spoon the rice mixture into two serving dishes. Top each portion with tablespoon of dessert topping.

Fluffy Orange Sundae

EXCHANGES PER SERVING: 1½ Fruit
10 Calories Optional

SERVES 4 (80 Calories per serving)

This refreshing fluffy jelly can be made in advance and kept in the refrigerator.

2 tablespoons gelatine

8 tablespoons boiling water

1pt 4fl oz (720ml) orange juice

2 teaspoons grated lemon zest

8fl oz (240ml) cold water

artificial sweetener to taste

20 raspberries (2½oz/75g) to garnish

Sprinkle the gelatine over the boiling water, stir and leave until dissolved. Stir the orange juice, lemon zest, cold water and sufficient sweetener to taste into the dissolved gelatine. Place the mixture into a mixing bowl and refrigerate for 1–2 hours until beginning to set. Remove the setting jelly from the refrigerator and whisk well, pour the frothy mixture into a serving bowl or glasses and return to the refrigerator until completely set. Garnish with the raspberries before serving.

SPAIN AND PORTUGAL

Fish for interesting recipes from the Iberian Peninsula. Spain and Portugal feature a wealth of seafood specialities, from which we have chosen Gambas con Salsa Verde and Gambas al Ajillo, as well as the Paella which features both shellfish and chicken. Paella is the Spanish national dish, always made with saffron coloured rice and several kinds of meat and fish depending on the region, as well as various other ingredients. 'Paella' is the Spanish word for the pan in which this dish is usually cooked and served.

Garlic, olives, olive oil and tomatoes are the most common ingredients of this cuisine. In fact, the enterprising Spanish are said to have invented tomato sauce. Portuguese cooking tends to be plainer, but it too depends on the same main ingredients. Portuguese Steak is a good example.

The Spanish and Portuguese taste for aromatic dishes goes well with a climate which is ideal for the production of fresh produce fully ripened in the sun. In a land of contrasts and extremes, Iberian cooking could only be robust and flavoursome.

As for the desserts, the superb fruits are often the most popular choice, but we have included here three luscious concoctions: the Tart Ibiza with wine and grapes, the Torta de Arroz, a delicious rice cake, and the Amor Frio, an orange-flavoured dessert with a creamy taste and texture.

Try our menu for a taste of summer!

MENU

Paella

tomato and onion salad

mixed pepper salad

Amor Frio

coffee

red wine

Gambas al Ajillo

SERVES 4 (140 Calories per serving)

Change a simple dish into something special with this hot garlic sauce.

3 garlic cloves, peeled

2 tablespoons olive oil

paprika

8oz (240g) large peeled prawns

2 tablespoons dry sherry

2 teaspoons lemon juice

salt and pepper

Finely chop 1 garlic clove and, using a pestle and mortar or a small bowl and the back of a spoon, mash the garlic to a paste. Gradually whisk in 2 teaspoons of oil, beating well until the mixture reaches the consistency of mayonnaise.

Heat the remaining oil in a medium-sized frying pan over a high heat. Add the remaining two garlic cloves and a sprinkling of paprika and saute until the garlic turns golden brown, about 1 minute. (Take care not to burn the garlic or it will spoil the flavour.) Remove and discard the garlic. Add the prawns to the hot oil and saute 1–2 minutes on each side. Add the sherry, lemon juice, salt and pepper and cook for 1 minute. Add the garlic and oil mixture and stir well to combine. Serve immediately.

EXCHANGES PER SERVING: 1½ Fat
2 Protein
10 Calories Optional

Tortilla Paisana

SERVES 2 (320 Calories per serving)

This is the Spanish version of the omelette. It is 'fried' first and then browned under a grill instead of folding in half and setting over a very high heat.

1 tablespoon vegetable oil

½ onion, thinly sliced

½ red pepper, seeded and cut into thin strips

6oz (180g) cooked potatoes, thinly sliced

1oz (30g) boiled ham, cut into thin strips

3oz (90g) asparagus spears, diced and blanched

2oz (60g) frozen peas, thawed

3 eggs, beaten

large pinch salt

large pinch paprika

Heat 1 teaspoon oil in a large non-stick frying pan, add the onion and pepper and saute gently for 2–3 minutes. Remove from the frying pan and set aside. Heat remaining oil, add the potatoes and top with the ham, asparagus, peas, onions and peppers. Season the eggs with the salt and paprika and pour into the frying pan. Cook over a medium heat until the bottom of the tortilla turns golden brown, 4–6 minutes. While the tortilla is cooking, preheat the grill on its highest setting and transfer the pan to the grill as soon as the base is golden brown. Grill until the eggs are set and beginning to brown. Ease the edges of the tortilla away from the pan with a spatula and carefully slide onto a warm serving plate.

EXCHANGES PER SERVING: 1½ Fat
1½ Vegetable
1 Bread
2 Protein

Top: Tortilla Paisana
Bottom: Amor Frio (p 213)

Basque Green Beans

EXCHANGES PER SERVING: 1½ Vegetable
½ Fat
½ Protein
10 Calories Optional

SERVES 4 (75 Calories per serving)

These crunchy beans served in a flavoursome sauce make an interesting vegetable accompaniment to a variety of dishes.

2 teaspoons olive oil

3–4 garlic cloves, finely chopped

6oz (180g) red pepper, seeded and sliced

2oz (60g) boiled ham, chopped

4fl oz (120ml) chicken stock

8 teaspoons dry sherry

2 teaspoons lemon juice

2 teaspoons chopped parsley

12oz (360g) whole green beans, blanched

salt and pepper

Heat the oil in a frying pan over a medium heat. Add the garlic and pepper and saute for 2–3 minutes until the pepper begins to soften. Stir in all the remaining ingredients and boil uncovered until the liquid is reduced by half and the beans are heated through, 2–3 minutes. Adjust the seasoning and serve.

Portuguese Steak

SERVES 4 (305 Calories per serving)

Serve this steak with a salad and potatoes or rice.

4–6 garlic cloves, finely chopped

2 teaspoons red wine vinegar

½ teaspoon pepper

4 × 5-oz (150-g) sirloin steaks

1 teaspoon olive oil

1 teaspoon margarine

4 × ½-oz (15-g) slices Parma ham

8fl oz (240ml) beef stock

8 teaspoons red wine

2 teaspoons lemon juice

Using a pestle and mortar or in a small bowl using the back of a spoon, mash the garlic, vinegar and pepper together to form a smooth paste. Spread an eighth of the mixture onto the four steaks. Preheat the grill on its highest setting. Transfer the steaks to the rack of the grill pan and grill for 4–5 minutes. Turn the steaks over and brush with the remaining garlic mixture, return to the grill until cooked according to taste.

While the steaks are cooking, heat the oil and margarine in a large frying pan. When hot and bubbling, add the Parma ham and saute for 30 seconds, transfer to a warm plate and keep warm. Add the stock, wine and lemon juice to the frying pan and bring to the boil. Reduce the heat and simmer gently, stirring occasionally for 2–3 minutes.

To serve, top each steak with a slice of Parma ham and pour a quarter of the sauce over each portion.

EXCHANGES PER SERVING: 4½ Protein
½ Fat
10 Calories Optional

Chicken Sofrito

SERVES 2 (285 Calories per serving)

This colourful dish is very tasty on its own and needs no more than plain boiled rice and fresh green beans as an accompaniment.

1 tablespoon olive oil

2 garlic cloves, finely chopped

3oz (90g) onion, chopped

3oz (90g) green pepper, seeded and chopped

14oz (420g) canned tomatoes, drained, reserve juice and chop tomatoes

6fl oz (180ml) chicken stock

1½oz (45g) mushrooms, sliced

1oz (30g) boiled ham, cut into thin strips

2 tablespoons sherry

1 teaspoon oregano

¼ teaspoon salt

large pinch paprika

9oz (270g) skinned and boned chicken breasts, each cut into 3 × ½-inch (1-cm) strips

4 pimento-stuffed green olives, sliced

Heat 1 teaspoon oil in a saucepan over a moderate heat. Add the garlic, onion and pepper and saute for 2–3 minutes until the onion is translucent. Stir in the remaining ingredients except the chicken and olives. Reduce the heat to low and simmer gently for 15 minutes, stirring occasionally.

While the tomato mixture is cooking, heat the remaining oil in a frying pan. Add the chicken and stir-fry until golden brown all over. Transfer the chicken to the sauce and stir in the sliced olives. Increase the heat and continue cooking until the chicken is cooked through and the sauce thickened, 5–6 minutes. Transfer to a warm serving plate.

EXCHANGES PER SERVING: 1½ Fat
3½ Vegetable
4 Protein
25 Calories Optional

Gambas Con Salsa Verde

SERVES 2 (85 Calories per serving)

Herbs and wine combine to give these skewered prawns a unique flavour.

½oz (15g) fresh parsley leaves, rinsed
4 tablespoons fresh coriander, rinsed
2 tablespoons water
1 tablespoon white wine
4 garlic cloves, chopped
2 teaspoons chopped shallots
2 teaspoons drained capers
2 teaspoons olive oil
1 teaspoon lemon juice
salt and pepper
8 Pacific prawns, about 6oz (180g)

Place all the ingredients, except the prawns, in a blender and process until smooth, scraping down the sides of the container as necessary.

Shell the prawns leaving the tail 'feathers' on. Starting at the tail end of each prawn, thread one prawn onto each of eight small skewers. Transfer the skewers to a non-stick baking sheet and grill for 1–2 minutes. Turn the prawns over and spread with an eighth of the green sauce, return to the grill for a further 1–2 minutes. Do not overcook or the prawns will toughen. Serve immediately.

EXCHANGES PER SERVING:	½ Vegetable
	1 Fat
	2 Protein
	10 Calories Optional

Paella

SERVES 4 (330 Calories per serving)

There are no hard and fast rules about making a paella but shellfish, chicken, rice and peppers are usually included in all recipes.

1 tablespoon olive oil

1 garlic clove, finely chopped

1 red or green pepper, or a mixture of both, seeded and cut into thin strips

1 onion, finely chopped

14oz (420g) skinned and boned chicken breasts, cut into ½-inch (1-cm) strips

2 tomatoes, peeled and chopped

4oz (120g) long grain rice

good pinch powdered saffron

approximately 12fl oz (360ml) boiling water

¼ teaspoon salt

4oz (120g) peeled prawns or 3oz (90g) peeled prawns and 8 unpeeled prawns

6oz (180g) frozen peas

8 large mussels, steamed

chopped parsley to garnish

Heat the oil in a saucepan, deep frying pan or paella pan. Add the garlic, peppers and onion and cook 2–3 minutes. Add the chicken and saute over a medium heat until the chicken loses its pink colour, stirring all the time. Stir in the tomatoes and rice and cook for a further 2 minutes. Stir in the saffron, boiling water and salt and cook for about 10 minutes. Add the peeled prawns and peas and cook for a further 5 minutes or until the rice is cooked through. Add the mussels and heat through. Sprinkle with the chopped parsley and if unpeeled prawns are to be included in the recipe, garnish with the eight unpeeled prawns.

EXCHANGES PER SERVING: ½ Fat
1½ Vegetable
4 Protein
1 Bread
15 Calories Optional

Torta de Arroz

SERVES 8 (280 Calories per serving)

An apricot glaze makes this Spanish rice cake special.

5oz (150g) skimmed milk powder made up to 1 pint 4fl oz (720ml) with cold water
1 pint (600ml) skimmed milk
4 teaspoons granulated sugar
1 tablespoon dry sherry
1 teaspoon grated orange zest
1 teaspoon vanilla flavouring
¾ teaspoon ground cinnamon
½ teaspoon grated lemon zest
¼ teaspoon ground nutmeg
¼ teaspoon salt
8oz (240g) long grain rice
1 teaspoon vegetable oil
4 eggs, separated
8 tablespoons low-calorie apricot jam
2 tablespoons desiccated coconut

Combine the milks, sugar, sherry, orange zest, vanilla flavouring, cinnamon, lemon zest, nutmeg and salt in a large saucepan. Bring to the boil over a moderate heat, stirring frequently. Reduce the heat to low, stir in the rice and cook uncovered, stirring from time to time until the rice is tender, 40–50 minutes. Remove from the heat and leave to cool.

Preheat the oven to 375°F, 190°C, Gas Mark 5. Lightly grease a non-stick 9-inch (23-cm) ring mould with the oil. Whisk the egg whites in a clean bowl until peaking. Stir the egg yolks into the rice mixture then gently fold in the whisked egg whites. Spoon into the prepared ring mould. Place the ring mould in a baking tin and pour hot water in to a depth of about 1½ inches (4cm). Bake in the centre of the preheated oven for 50–60 minutes until the cake springs back when pressed lightly. Remove the ring mould from the water bath and allow to cool for 5 minutes. Invert the cake onto the serving plate and leave to cool for a further 10–15 minutes.

Heat the apricot jam in a small saucepan over a low heat, stirring frequently. Drizzle the melted apricot jam over the cake and sprinkle with desiccated coconut.

EXCHANGES PER SERVING: ¾ Milk
1 Bread
½ Protein
65 Calories Optional

Paella (p 209)

Tart Ibiza

SERVES 8 (195 Calories per serving)

A Spanish wine tart, beautifully decorated with luscious grapes.

FOR THE PASTRY:

3oz (90g) plain flour

pinch salt

8 teaspoons margarine

4 tablespoons low-fat natural yogurt

1 tablespoon flour for rolling out pastry

FOR THE FILLING:

4 eggs, separated

2oz (60g) or 4 tablespoons caster sugar

3 tablespoons lemon juice

1½ teaspoons grated lemon zest

4fl oz (120ml) dry white wine

12oz (360g) large green grapes, halved and seeded

To prepare the pastry case: Preheat the oven to 375°F, 190°C, Gas Mark 5. Mix the flour and salt together in a mixing bowl. Rub in the margarine until the mixture resembles coarse breadcrumbs. Stir in the yogurt and mix thoroughly to form a dough. Using the extra tablespoon of flour, roll out the pastry to a thickness of about ⅛ inch (2.5mm). Transfer the pastry to a 9-inch (23-cm) flan dish or pie plate. Prick the bottom and sides of the pastry crust and bake in the preheated oven for 15–18 minutes until lightly browned.

To prepare the filling: Mix together the egg yolks, sugar, lemon juice, lemon zest and wine. Cook the egg and wine mixture in the top of a double saucepan over simmering water. Stir constantly until the mixture is thick enough to thinly coat the back of the spoon.

Whisk the egg whites in a bowl until peaking. Gently fold the whites into the yolk mixture. Spoon the mixture into the baked crust and return to the oven for about 15 minutes until golden brown. Remove from the oven and allow to cool on a wire rack. Decoratively arrange the grapes over the tart prior to serving.

EXCHANGES PER SERVING: 1 Fat
½ Protein
½ Fruit
90 Calories Optional

Amor Frio

SERVES 4 (160 Calories per serving)

This delicious Spanish orange pudding will turn any dinner into a memorable meal.

2 medium oranges, peeled

2 tablespoons dry sherry

10fl oz (300ml) skimmed milk

2 eggs, separated

2 tablespoons caster sugar

1 tablespoon gelatine

¼ teaspoon ground cinnamon

2 teaspoons lemon juice

1 teaspoon grated orange zest

4 tablespoons whipped dessert topping

pinch of salt

orange zest to garnish

Divide the oranges into segments, removing all membranes and catching any juices. Cut the orange segments into ½-inch (1-cm) pieces. Sprinkle the sherry over the cut segments, cover and refrigerate.

Heat the milk, egg yolks, sugar, gelatine and cinnamon in a double saucepan. Stir over gently simmering water until the mixture thickens slightly, about 15 minutes. Pour the thickened custard into a bowl, allow to cool, then chill in the refrigerator for about 30 minutes.

Stir the orange and sherry mixture, lemon juice and orange zest into the chilled custard. Fold in the whipped dessert topping. Add the pinch of salt to the egg whites and whisk until peaking, carefully fold into the custard. Spoon the mixture into serving glasses, cover and refrigerate for about 3 hours or until set. Decorate with the orange zest.

EXCHANGES PER SERVING: ½ Fruit
¼ Milk
½ Protein
70 Calories Optional

MENU EXCHANGE TOTALS

Here is a list of the total number of Exchanges *per person* for each of the menus at the start of each of the 14 chapters, *not* including the drinks.

Australia and New Zealand	(page 11)	3 Fruit	3½ Vegetable	¾ Milk
		½ Bread	3 Fat	6 Protein
		230 Optional Calories Banked		
Belgium, The Netherlands and Luxembourg	(page 25)	1 Fruit	4 Vegetable	2 Bread
		3 Fat	6 Protein	
		65 Optional Calories		
The British Isles	(page 39)	1 Fruit	5½ Vegetable	1 Bread
		3 Fat	5½ Protein	
		30 Optional Calories		
Central and Eastern Europe	(page 55)	1 Fruit	3 Vegetable	2 Bread
		2 Fat	4 Protein	
		100 Optional Calories		
China	(page 69)	1 Fruit	2½ Vegetable	1½ Bread
		1½ Fat	4 Protein	
		75 Optional Calories		
France	(page 83)	1 Fruit	5 Vegetable	1 Bread
		2 Fat	4½ Protein	
		40 Optional Calories		

Germany	(page 99)	3 Fruit 2 Fat 55 Optional Calories	2½ Vegetable 4 Protein	1 Bread
Greece	(page 113)	2 Fruit 2 Fat 30 Optional Calories	4½ Vegetable 4 Protein	1 Bread
India	(page 127)	2½ Fruit 1¾ Fat 40 Optional Calories	3 Vegetable 4 Protein	3 Bread
Italy	(page 141)	1 Fruit 1 Bread 150 Optional Calories	3 Vegetable 2 Fat	¼ Milk 6 Protein
North America	(page 155)	1 Fruit 3 Fat 85 Optional Calories	5 Vegetable 6 Protein	2½ Bread
Russia	(page 171)	1 Fruit 2½ Fat 115 Optional Calories	4½ Vegetable 6 Protein	2 Bread
Scandinavia	(page 185)	1½ Fruit 1¼ Bread 80 Optional Calories	4½ Vegetable 2½ Fat	½ Milk 4 Protein
Spain and Portugal	(page 199)	½ Fruit 1 Bread 85 Optional Calories	4½ Vegetable ½ Fat	¼ Milk 4½ Protein

INDEX

Numbers in italics refer to illustrations

D

E

F

G

H

I

J

K

L

NOTES